# Jack, Russell and Me (And, Philippe!)

R. A. PACE

iUniverse

# JACK, RUSSELL AND ME (AND, PHILIPPE!)

*iUniverse books may be ordered through booksellers or by contacting:*

*iUniverse*
*1663 Liberty Drive*
*Bloomington, IN 47403*
*www.iuniverse.com*
*844-349-9409*

*Because of the dynamic nature of the Internet, any web addresses or links contained in this book may have changed since publication and may no longer be valid. The views expressed in this work are solely those of the author and do not necessarily reflect the views of the publisher, and the publisher hereby disclaims any responsibility for them.*

*Any people depicted in stock imagery provided by Getty Images are models, and such images are being used for illustrative purposes only. Certain stock imagery © Getty Images.*

*ISBN: 978-1-6632-3105-5 (sc)*
*ISBN: 978-1-6632-3106-2 (e)*

*Library of Congress Control Number: 2021925755*

*Print information available on the last page.*

*iUniverse rev. date:   01/04/2022*

# PART ONE

# PROLOGUE

WHEN I WAS YOUNG, I HAD ANY ANIMALS. NOW, WAIT, what did I just write? Were they property? No. I should correct myself: I cared for many animals. I was a child, but I felt that, as an adult, I was going to be the best caretaker whomever lived. Maybe I was overreaching. I ended up being a caretaker, but not the best. But, isn't that how all dog mothers feel? I had plenty of time, and practice with animals. Dogs, birds, spiders, and, of course, a ferret sprinkled my childhood with joy. I could never tell if it was equally elating for them. All I knew was that I loved animals, and wanted to have one, maybe two myself.

So, when I was 22, I did. I adopted two jack russell terriers for 100 pounds from a couple living in King's Lynn, England. And, as all stories about animals go, there was much joy, as stated, (which would evade me otherwise), but a sad ending. They simply don't live as long as we do, but, for me, Jack and Russell, the names of my JRT's, will have me as their dog mother for eternity. So, when I was young, I cared for animals, with much love, and patience. And, this of course, is their story.

# CHAPTER ONE

THE FIRST TIME I LAID EYES ON JACK AND RUSSELL, I WAS elated. Their cuteness as puppies ignited a joyful sensation that lit up the office on the military base that I was stationed at.

"Here they are."

"Oh, my God, they're so cute. Hey, little fellas."

"You have to be careful. They will wiggle, and run away."

"Oh, my goodness. I'm noticing."

"Yeah, I wanted to keep all of them, but my husband wouldn't let me."

"Oh, really?"

"Yeah."

"Okay. 100 pounds."

"Yes, it will help with gas. We live in King's Lynn. I was actually almost home when you called. I turned around, of course."

"Oh, I'm sorry."

"No, it's fine. Take care of them."

"I will."

"Okay, well, I've got to head out."

"Okay, take care."

"See 'ya around."

I couldn't wait to see my new little puppies in action. With the permission of my tech sergeant, I unlocked the cages in the office, and out they went. Russell wandered off, and urinated on the carpet, and Jack wagged his was toward me, sniffing, and licking. I chased after Russell, after petting Jack, and cleaned up the accident.

The new darlings in my life were posted to a network for sales transactions. I only made one request—that they both be the same gender. I didn't know what a Jack Russell Terrier was at twenty-two, but, my goodness, did I learn.

After playing with Jack and Russell for thirty minutes, or so, we loaded up into the car, and headed to RAF Mildenhall's base exchange, where I would purchase food, and bedding, and, of course, toys.

"Are you just going to leave them here?"

"Yeah, the clerk said that they can't go in."

""Oh, we'll watch them, won't we kids?"

"Thank you, sir. I won't be long."

With a limited budget, I still bought the best quality items, and hurried back to my little ones being puppy-sat by an Air Force captain, and his family.

"Thank you so much for watching them, sir. Thank you."

"You're welcome."

"What are their names?"

"Oh, I haven't named them yet. I just got them today."

"Well, they're cute little buggers."

"Yes, they are. Again, thank you."

"Okay, take care, and good luck."

With Jack and Russell in the car, I played Mozart to soothe their terrier nerves."

"Okay, sweeties, we're home."

Home was Bury St. Edmunds, a flat in a lower income neighborhood mainly occupied by the elderly. My flat was ample in size, but outdated. All the same, it was a safe home for my growing puppies.

"Okay, here's your bed, little ones."

The two little puppies immediately cuddled up, and went to sleep. Then, midnight came.

"Howl!"

I woke up, and put both puppies in my bed. With their little heads on my pillow, they fell asleep. And, that was my first day with Jack and Russell.

---

Naming a puppy is difficult for some. However, Russell made it easy. He got excited while listening to a punk rock band.

"I was thinking of naming them after rock stars."

"Oh, don't do that. It will be bad karma for them. What about Jack and Russell?"

"Oh, my God, that's so cute. I think that I will."

So, with the help of the Ministry of Defense, Jack, and Russel it was.

---

I had never heard of a dog warden before Jack and Russell. Like anyone in the military, I went to work early in the morning, pressured to arrive at least ten minutes prior to my tour of duty. Of course, Jack and Russell did not like this. So, each time I left in the morning, they would howl at length in the back garden. I loved them, so I ignored it, thinking that it was cute. My rich neighbors didn't. One evening, I went through the mail for the day, and found a letter from that wealthy neighboring community. It was not kind. Amid the abrasive langue was a threat to call the dog warden over "your barking dogs." So, it was time for Jack, and Russell to stay inside, and miss the nice summer days.

—————————

As it goes with jack russell terriers, wiggly is not the word. On our first walk on a leash, I chose to take the little ones behind the flat on a footpath bordering an open field.

"Oh, look at the little angels."

"Yeah, they're my saviors."

"What are their names?"

"Jack, and Russell."

"Oh, how cute."

Then, excitement came into Jack and Russell's little bodies. After meeting the two elderly women, Jack darted off, escaping his collar. So, we were off to the races. Naturally, Russell pulled away, and also escaped. I ran as fat as I could, chasing after them. Eventually, exhausted, I snagged both of them, and tightened their collars. Our first trip walking had become a busy run-and-play outing. I finally knew about why my fellow airmen kept saying that jack russell terriers can get away easily, and run off (making their mother have a nervous breakdown.)

---

Given the complaints about barking, I kept Jack and Russell in the carpeted foyer of my flat—one of my mistakes. They had plenty of toys, food, and water, and special bedding that I routinely had to replace. Then, one evening, I came home to it—the entire carpeted foyer, and stairwell turned to shreds. Jack and Russell were good about urinating, and defecating on the piddle squares, but they were not so good about their teething anxiety. So, for six hundred pounds, the carpet was replaced, and the dogs were again brought out into the garden before work, staying in a shed to seek comfort, and shelter during rainy days.

---

In spite of nearly everyone thinking that Jack and Russell weren't disciplined, I thought that they were adorable. I tried to make good with the neighborhood by adding roses to the front garden, as well as landscaping both front, and back gardens. In the back, I planted bushes, and decided to line the walkway with tulips, and various other flowers. Russell decided to help. As I put in a yellow tulip, Russell came over, and pulled the tulip right out of the ground.

"Oh, look at that, a master gardener."

"Russell, no, the tulip stays in the ground, sweet thing."

"He doesn't like your garden."

With that, the overseer backed away from daily complaints, and decided to help dog-sit Jack, and Russell while I was away at work.

———————

While at work, I often thought about Jack and Russell, but didn't call the overseer, trusting that all was well.

"Rebecca, I have some bad news for you. The little ones escaped into the flats, and I had to run after them. They almost got away, and ran into the street. Now had they done that, they wouldn't be with us."

"Oh, my God! Okay, I already called my mom because of the letter. They're going back to the United States in October. I just need a month to get everything together."

"Oh, thank God. I didn't want to have to tell you to get rid of them."

"Oh, no. I understand. They're going home."

———————

I made sure that Jack, and Russell would go on their first plane trip in style, buying them jackets for the cold air. They were sedated, and in one kennel.

"Ma'am, you can't fly two dogs in one kennel."

"Oh, but I have to send them home. I don't want to give them up."

"Well, you can purchase a kennel from one of our associates."

"Oh, okay, I'll do that."

"Right, here's the number. You can just phone him, and he'll bring it to you just out front."

"Okay, thank you."

"Mom, stay here with them. I'll be just out front."

"Okay, hurry up. We only have an hour."

Sixty pounds later, I had another dog kennel. Both Jack and Russell met standards for the transport for animals. I cried. In fact, I cried a lot, almost embarrassing myself. But, they were safe, and comfortable. In my mind, I only had to wait three months. I'd put in the early separation for education. I was going home. My mother was elated. When my mother got home, the wait was exhausting, and Jack, and Russell didn't wake up until she arrived home. Everything had changed. I was now mature, and a dog mother, and my babies were across the pond. Now, I just wanted to go home. Jack and Russell waited.

# CHAPTER TWO

THREE MONTHS WENT BY. JACK AND RUSSELL WERE IN Zebulon, North Carolina with my parents who also had a fenced yard, and a dog door. They were safe, and still waiting. After a month, I thought that I was going home. Stop loss hit. I had to wait eight months, reaching almost a five year active duty enlistment. Of course, May 11th, 2003, I finally went home. I walked into the house, and heard little claws clicking against the marble flooring.

"Hey, little babies. How are you?"

"Sorry. They got fat," my mother said.

"That's okay."

"I told mom to stop feeding them so much," my father said.

"Oh, look at the little whiskers."

"Yeah, they're busy bodies."

"Did they have whiskers before?"

"Yes, Rebecca. Why would you ask that?"

Home, I was still traumatized, and rapidly becoming mentally ill. Naturally, I was still determined to raise Jack and Russell in good health, and with lots of affection.

As with any darling pets, vet visits are necessary. Jack, Russell and me had moved to Sylva, North Carolina where I would attend Western Carolina University in Cullowhee, just down the road. Jack and Russell did not take to the move kindly, even though we lived on a nice piece of property with a pond. The residence was also a minute from the Tuckaseegee River.

"Grrr."

"Oh, Russell, stop. We need to see if you're sick."

"That little dog is just in a bad mood."

"Yes, he is. I don't know what's wrong. We moved from Zebulon."

"It must be the move."

"Yeah, I thought that they would like the mountains better."

"They will."

———————————

Every day, Jack, Russell and me had one routine: a morning walk to the property's pond, and an afternoon walk to the river. Each morning, I would get out the long zippy leashes, and would coax the little ones down to the pond.

"Come on, Jack. Come on, Russell. Come here, sweeties."

The dogs would always oblige, knowing that it was their favorite thing to do. So, we would walk a few hundred yards to the pond, and both Jack, and Russell would go fishing, bark at the birds, and, sometimes, even swim. Then, I would go off to class, and they would sing, howling for mommy to stay home. Fortunately, not a point of annoyance to the neighbors.

In the afternoon, I would rest, then leash up Jack, and Russell for their one mile stroll along the side of the river. Only one day did some complain, rudely, suggesting that they owned the road along the river. Mostly, the walk were just what the dogs wanted, and needed. Their favorite activities were chasing snakes, and frogs, rock hopping, and the ultimate adventure was tracking the blue heron— the most majestic of indigenous birds. Alas, their walk had to end, and with bellies full of river water, they would nestle in for the evening.

---

Many times, I wondered about the road to the Blue Ridge Parkway, and, one day, I chose to drive down it, toward Cherokee. The doges did not mind. It seemed as though we were driving for hours. I wondered if there were any trails. Finally, after 30 minutes of driving around mountains on a winding roadway, there was a very developed outlet to Waterrock Knob.

We got out of the car. The dogs were ecstatic. Following the crowd, we walked up a paved footpath ascending to an outlook with breathtaking views.

"Look at that, Jack and Russell. Look."

The dogs both danced around, and we pressed on, hiking through brush on a dirt path. The trail's switchback was a long trek up the mountain, then full of rocks that Jack, and Russell had to jump up on. They didn't mind. They continued to pant, and smile.

When we reached the second summit, we looked out to see a panoramic picture of the Great Smokey Mountains.

"Look, boys, look."

Jack, and Russell both barked. Still excited, I took in the view, and all of us descended back to the car lot where Jack and Russell both got a treat for their very first American (home) hike.

———————

Jack and Russell enjoyed many hiking trips beyond their first adventure. At least three days a week, we left studying, and naps for the Blue Ridge Parkway, going both left to Cherokee, and right toward Asheville. Long trails, and short trails, Jack, and Russell simply loved it. Our great hike was always in the Wilderness, particularly Sam Knob. No one could say that we all weren't active, and enjoying the mountains. Of course, Jack and Russell had the energy to run, hike, and climb—they were still under two years old. And, with that age, they had moments, as it always goes with young adult dogs, of bad behavior.

———————

Each day, I would head off to my classes, I did not know about what was happening with Jack and Russell until neighbors informed me that they were getting into very violent fights. I had no yard for them to walk in, so they were outside on the porch. And, as it is with jack russell terriers, I most certainly could not let them wander free, and potentially run into the road, or encounter a larger dog.

I had seen them fight, sometimes drawing blood. One time, Russell went into such a frenzy that he bit me. His eyes got big, as though he knew that he had done something wrong, so I only bopped his nose as punishment.

Barking was the other complaint. I got so frustrated with the constant, violent barking that I screamed at both Jack and Russell one night. It only made it worse. So, as with every new dog mother, I bought every book that I could find on how to train two unruly dog children. With time, the training worked, and all of us were happy again.

# CHAPTER THREE

COMING INTO ADULTHOOD, I DECIDED TO TAKE JACK AND Russell to the beach, the Outer Banks, for a winter trip. They were about four, but still full of energy, and life, so I booked a pet-friendly hotel room; the trip to the beach from Zebulon was long, but worth the drive.

"Hello, I have a room for the night. Is it okay for my dogs to be in the lobby?"

"Oh, yes, of course."

"Okay, great. Here's my card, and reservation number."

The room was on the bottom floor, with a door to the outside, grassy area for dogs to relieve themselves. There was no view, so once all of the luggage was unpacked, we went to the walkway leading to the beach.

The sound of the ocean roared as we came closer to the water. Jack and Russell both pulled during the short walk, paused, then danced, and ran when we came to the open beach. Even I was elated; I could feel their happiness, which, for a time, lifted my depression.

"Come on, Jack, come to the water. It'll be fun. Come on, Russell. Good boy."

The dogs ran around the waves coming to the shore, and Russell decided that it was terrifying, so he darted away from the second wave toward the dunes. Fortunately, he was on a leash.

"Oh, Russell. It's not that bad. Come on."

Russell refused, so, for a thirty minute walk, Jack enjoyed the water, and Russell pulled himself as far away from the waves as possible.

With love, we went to eateries, but ended up buying groceries instead, groceries that included special dog treats. I didn't want Jack and Russell to wait while I dined, so we ate in the hotel room, as I was a vegetarian, and could not eat fast food.

Nestled in. we walked out to the beach several times, and finally retired. I could tell that Jack, and Russell (even Russell) were enjoying themselves due to their dog smiles. Alas, with all things, we left the next morning, and headed back to Zebulon, to the house, and the yard. All of us had felt the good feeling of having gone on a small trip, with a big reward: joy.

———————————

When school started again, when I had decided to go on to graduate school, I rented out a house in Cullowhee, just five minutes away from Western Carolina University. The short drive would afford me time to check in on the dogs, and not have to worry about dog fights. For a month, Jack, Russell and me lived out of a hotel room in Sylva, but when the house was ready, I could tell that Jack, and Russell liked their new abode. My first item of business was a fence. Then, I was able to arrange the house in such a way that it was perfect, feng shui perfect, with new recycled dishes, and organic bedding. Jack and Russell were happy, and had almost immediately taken to chasing lizards. The road I lived on was rarely travelled, so we even had a good walking path. It was so remote, I could also let Jack and Russell chase rabbits into the woods. They always came back, and I knew that we had found a good home with good karma.

---

Even though both Jack and Russell loved their new residence, it was situated on the side of a mountain, and prone to outages of all kinds. This was normal for the area. However, Jack discovered something else: lightening.

One day, a typical storm passed through, and then, crack! Lightening hit just outside of the backdoor.

"It's okay, Jack. It's okay."

Jack was shaking so severely that it looked like a seizure. So, every time lightening hit somewhere close by, Jack would shake. Russell, well, Russell would nap.

---

On many occasions, we would have fun, and not bad fun, good fun. One night, I had begun a graduate school thesis for creative writing, and because the outline, and voice were completed, I decided to play music, and dance.

"Come on, Jack. Let's dance. Come here, Russell, you, too."

One-by-one, I took Jack and Russell into my arms, and twirled them around, with their eyes growing larger, and tails ceasing to wag. So, for the night, we danced, and wiggled, and wagged around, and, in spite of graduate school stress, we had fun; fun had for Jack and Russell in adulthood.

# CHAPTER FOUR

ADULTHOOD PASSED INTO MATURE ADULTHOOD, AND I got a teaching assignment in Korea. My first thought was, 'Can I take the dogs?' My second thought was, 'Will they allow dogs in the apartment?' Having fished through offers, I decided on Uljin, Korea, a small town on the coast. It was an attractive offer with everything that Jack and Russell liked. So, I got on the phone with the airline after having accepted the position.

"Hi, I need to bring my two dogs to South Korea. Can I book their flight now?"

"I'm sorry, but we don't fly pets during the summer due to the extreme heat. Some animals have died."

"Oh, okay, I see. Can I book a future flight for them? And, when?"

"In September, we allow animals to travel. Will you be bringing anyone with you?"

"No, I was going to just go by myself."

"Well, there's an airplane policy of one pet per passenger."

"Oh, okay."

"Can you have someone fly with you?"

"I can't afford to fly two people."

"Well, I'm sorry, it's airline policy."

"Okay, thanks anyway."

I was devastated. So, for months, I was in Korea trying to stay for six months to stabilize my resume. Five months in, I couldn't take the distance from my dogs, so I left just shy of the six month mark. I'd read horror stories on the Internet anyway. "Dogs don't handle foreign travel well," one post noted. "Strands of viruses do not affect native pets, but potentially kill foreign pets," another warned. So, again, I went home, and went to Marion, North Carolina where my parents had purchased a vacation home that would become their retirement home, and where Jack and Russell had been mostly staying.

"Jack ran down the road toward I-40 looking for you, Rebecca. It's a good thing that you came home," my father said.

"Yes, it is. I couldn't take not being with them."

And, I never tried international work assignments again.

———————

Russel, and Jack always thought that they were big dogs with great powers, and the same spunk. Jack, back in Zebulon, would catapult himself off of the deck while chasing after squirrels—one, he caught. Russell, on day, did the same.

"What's this? Oh my, God, you're bleeding. Okay, let me call the vet."

Russell kept smiling, and panting, even though a trace of blood was coming from his paw.

"Hi, yes, I have a dog who is bleeding from his paw. Do you have an available appointment, like, soon?"

"Yeah, sure, bring him right in."

Russell's paw's bleeding got worse, so I wrapped it with a bandage.

"Okay, Russell just stay calm. Mommy's taking you to the vet."

The vet Russell normally went to was booked, so we were one town over where Russell had never been, so I was a little nervous.

"Okay, let's see what we've got here."

"It just wouldn't stop bleeding," I said.

"Okay, Mr. Russell, it looks like you ripped your toe nail clear out of there, and even broke your bone. I'm going to have to get him in the back to bandage him up, which you'll have to change, and we can give him some medicine for the pain. That's right, that's got to hurt little fella."

"Okay, sure, yeah."

So, with a large bandage, and pain pills, Russell was just fine, but now toeless on one paw's claw.

———————————

Time went by, and Jack, Russell and me were forced into low income housing due to, partly, a deep recession, and, partly also due to my mental illness. I had been diagnosed with schizophrenia, but wanted to live independently, away from my parents, so the dogs moved, and I tried my best to pick a comfortable abode. Unfortunately, the residence was roach infested, and just off of a busy road—something unsafe for Jack and Russell. One day, I realized just how unsafe the proximity was.

"Jack, Russell, no. Come back."

As I was moving in new furniture, Jack and Russell took off, running across the road with me right behind them. I just ran, blocking traffic, and chasing them into a neighborhood across the street.

"Come here. Come here, now. Good boys. Good boys."

"They got away from you, didn't they?"

"Yes, they sure did."

"Here, you can sit in the back of my truck. I'll take ya'll home. Where do you live?"

"Just across the street. Oh, God, thank you."

"Okay, hop on."

After a dangerous ordeal, all was well again. We were home, and I remembered to close the door from that point on.

---

After I'd go to appointments at the Veterans Affairs Hospital, I would take Jack and Russel for a walk. Almost jealous, we'd walk to Duke University, to the art museum, and back. I'd lost my mind, but Jack and Russell were reminded that it was okay with the walks to the campus. The gardens were their favorite places to be. But, we felt that it wasn't right, wasn't an appropriate place for two terriers, and a mentally ill mother. So, we moved.

---

At first, I was unsure about whether or not a move to Marion, to the farm would work out for all of us, given the reality that the mountains were expensive. Jack and Russell greeted the farm by running alongside, and in neighboring properties, so I once again put Jack and Russell on leashes, and simply walked them around the property. It wasn't a perfect situation, but my symptoms reduced, and the dogs finally started to calm down. However, it was my parents' farm, so, with great reserve, we moved to Asheville to endure apartment living—again.

———————

Apartment dwelling is not comfortable for people, so Jack and Russell immediately let me know that they were bored, felt cramped, and wanted to go back to the farm. We didn't. Instead, they went on walks, hikes, and took regular trips to pet stores that allowed dogs. Most of the time, we laid on the bed, and cuddled. For years, it went like this, and, then, one day, I took Russell to the vet for a cold that he had.

"I have some bad news."

"Okay."

"Russell's blood sugar is above 500. There are options. I can treat him here, but the emergency pet hospital can be more aggressive."

"What does that mean?"

"He has diabetes."

"Oh, okay. Well, I'd rather treat him more aggressively."

So, after a hefty bill, Russell was treated. We all moved to what became home. Then, I took Jack to the vet in Marion.

"Jack's liver enzymes are elevated."

"Okay."

"So, we went to ultrasound his liver . . ."

"Oh, okay, well . . ."

"He just has to stay here today, and you can pick him up around four o'clock."

"Okay, yes, we'll do that. It's okay, Mr. Jack."

The day went by. Jack was diagnosed with cirrhosis of the liver. Russell was a full blown diabetic with insulin shots, and eye drops. Now, Jack was on liver medicine, and seizure pills. They had aged right before my eyes. Both now ate prescription food. I would go into more debt each month, but I still bought everything that they needed. Russell had endured three years sick, and now Jack was sick. Russell was blind, however, so I literally carried him around for most of the day. Writing was the only job that I could do, so both Jac, and Russell received 24/7 care. There was no longer a need for leashes; both dogs were geriatric, and blind, or nearly blind. The final days were near, but I was in denial. I made weekly trips to the vet to purchase care items. I believed that they could live until twenty years of age, but, as everyone knows, dogs usually do not.

# CHAPTER FIVE

FOR 15 YEARS, I CARED FOR JACK AND RUSSELL. THEN, THE bad days came. Russell would urinate on the bed; Jack would defecate on the floor. In spite of their bad health, both dogs would go on energetic sprees. But, I was always reminded of their age. We no longer walked. Depression was setting in for all of us. Jack was having daily seizures, so I was certain that he would be the first to pass. I was wrong.

One night, Russell simply urinated, and whined the entire night, while also having diabetic seizures. By morning, he was howling, and violently seizing. There was no longer hope.

"Okay, Russell. Just let go."

I held Russell in my arms as my father drove him, on a Sunday, to the only open animal hospital. He was in pain. For an hour, he howled. When we arrived, the vet confirmed that there was nothing that could be done.

"Okay, years ago, they called it 'putting them to sleep,' because they literally go to sleep."

One injection went in, after Russell was sedated. He stopped whining. The second shot went in.

"Okay, he's gone. You can spend as much time with him as you want."

"No, I can't. I'm not doing so well myself."

"Okay."

I saw Russell's lifeless body, and began to shake. I could no longer hold back my pain. I cried that day, and for weeks to come. Obsessively, I took care of Jack, who was now held for those three years.

"I miss him, too, Jack."

With a passion for my remaining son, I cared for Jack, and we resumed hikes, and walks, with my nervous uncertainty.

---

Each roll of the skin pushed up as I lifted Jack into the air, his white fur shedding with my touch; his black, and brown face staring back at me with brown eyes deadest on mine.

"Whee!" I said.

Jack dangling for a moment, put his ears down, and reached for the floor safely. Wagging, he shook, and then scurried away.

"Russell, come here, Russell. Good boy."

Russell's body weight was heavier, and his legs shorter, with brown fur, and a blackish face.

"Grrr."

"Okay, Russell, I'll put you down."

It was midnight. I woke up. Both Jack and Russell's heads were on the blue sateen pillow, with their little bodies extended under the duvet.

"Good boys. Sweet things."

The hue of night had lulled them to sleep. Snoring, I rested my head, and watched them as they slept.

---

"Look at those tails. Tails wagging in the wind."

Jack and Russel were on their first strenuous hike going back to the car, calm, and swishing to every clip of their claws, smiling, and focusing on the footpath while I focused on them.

"You must take really good care of them," a hiker said.

"Yes, I guess that I do," I responded.

---

I looked back to the backseat of my care where Jack and Russell sat, smiling, panting, and expressing pant with their little barks. They had had their first adventure in an American pet store in which they got food, treats, toys, and a bed.

"Good boys. Good boys. Now, here's your treat," I said.

Eager to taste the treat, Jack took the green bone from my hand, placed it on the backseat, and then whipped back to try and take Russell's treat.

"Oh, no, Jack. Silly thing. Here, Russell.

I calmed them both.

---

"Okay, we made it. Wow. Look at that."

Russell barked, and smiled, panting, and sitting down. Jack wandered to the edge of the summit. We had made it to Shining Rock, a trail that lead to a 360 view of the Blue Ridge Parkway.

# EPILOGUE

AT THE SUMMIT, OUR SUMMIT, I DIDN'T WANT TO GO. I didn't want to let go. Jack had had a seizure. I was tired. Russell's ashes were tied tight in a bag. We had hiked into the Wilderness to Shining Rock.

"Come here, Jack. Come here."

While the trail was only a three mile loop, Jack did not want to finish either. We came to a grassy opening just at the foot of the main knoll. I opened Russell's box, exposing the bad with ashes. I closed the box, walked with Jack back to the trailhead, crying periodically.

"I miss him, too, Jack. I miss him, too. It's okay."

And, with knowing that I had tried, that I had given Russell everything, I let it go, looking at Jack, looking at the present forming memories, at the reality of having cared for two dogs for fifteen years, at the realization of having loved, at my Jack sitting right in front of me, at a chance to finalize getting it right. And, for all the affection that Jack and Russell had given me, I never felt alone, and always felt alive. I had been given more, and I had loved more.

---

Russell passed in August. It is now January of the New Year, and Jack is still alive. Initially, I bathed Jack with attention. We went on long walks, and he was served human meals in addition to luxury dog food. But, in time, Jack's seizures worsened, so he is now housebound, and unable to go outside for extensive periods of time. I still take him for rides, however. He is on three medications now, as well—one for his heart, one for his liver, and one for seizures. I had to return him to his medical prescription diet, which he does not like as much, but it will keep him alive. If Jack makes a lap around the field on the farm, that amounts to exercise. He still walks without great difficulty, but cannot hear, and cannot see well either. In time, his health will deteriorate farther, and I am prepared for another day at the emergency vet, but pray that he survives another six months. Losing Russell was hard, but losing both dogs will undo me. It's only a matter of time before Jack's last days come. I can only try to be a good dog mother, and do that very thing.

# PART TWO

# 1/4/16

I MISSED THE FIRST TWO, OR THREE DAYS OF JOURNALING due to a mishap in my sleeping schedule resulting from the common cold. With that noted, I would like to begin my journaling efforts.

Jack, the primarily white jack russell terrier, suffers from occasional seizures, obesity, and bad teeth. Russell, the brown jack russell terrier, ails from diabetes, blindness, cataracts, which Jack also suffers from, and glaucoma. Both are loved, and both reside in Marion, North Carolina, in my parents' house, due to financial reasons following the loss of my job, and high rent in Asheville. We do very little now, in January, but plans for good health, and rehabilitation are on the horizon. My goal: to take both Jack and Russell, both ill, hiking in their old playing ground, Sam Knob. How to do this with arthritic, geriatric dogs? Lots, and lots of walking. For instance, today, Jack and Russell walked around my parents' farm six times, no three (but, getting there!). I went around six times, a mile. I should note that I am a schizophrenic, complex PTSD-er, and major depression depressive who is morbidly obese. Jack and Russell? Only slightly obese. So, is this venture for myself, or them? Probably them. And, to encourage good health, by the way, I will be following good, old Ben Franklin's daily schedule as first published in his autobiography. Five o'clock in the morning. Ten o'clock in the evening (retire), etc. So, back to Jack and Russell. We have high hopes: hiking, tennis ball chasing, and, alas, good health. Although I failed to follow any schedule today, I hope that tomorrow will lend itself to a good wake-up call, and handsome schedule that will live up to the set standards I have deemed to be as healthy as possible.

As for today, what has been healthy? Jack and Russell were woken up at ten thirty in the morning, too late. They ate, but Russell mainly ate another dog's food. He received his insulin, eye drops, and supplements. Jack received a plain meal. Mainly, the boys laid in bed. But, Jack and Russell were roused to activity mid-day, when they did their half-mile walk around the field. More tomorrow.

# 1/6/16

AM I A GOOD DOG MOTHER, I OFTEN WONDER? Detoxifying from a year of drunkenness, I realize that I am not the ideal candidate to rehabilitate two geriatric jack russell terriers. But, I'm all that they have. Eye drops, and insulin, prescription food, and supplements, slow walk, and careful nail clippings, all of these thing entail Jack, and Russell's care, and daily care at that. Jack, still able to see, is easier to care for, while Russell requires intensive, minute-to-minute attention. He cannot see, and is arthritic with a bulging disk in his back. Jack has degeneration in his spine, but is still spritely. Yesterday, they both spent a great deal of time outside while I helped my parents unload gravel for an extended parking area. They seemed to enjoy it, but it's not enough. As I detox due to sobriety, and veganism, I feel tired, and heavy. While I have lost five pounds, I'm still 253.6 pounds today. I have a lot of problems, basically. I have Unemployed, disabled, and poverty-stricken. I have lofty goals: nurse assisting to pre-medical schooling to medical school. I've failed to engage any part of those dreams, however. But, this book is now about me, it's about Jack and Russell, my two first loves. They were adopted in 2002, when I was serving as an enlisted woman in the United States Air Force overseas. Today, they are children, my children. I spent over a decade practicing mothing by raising two jack russell terrier mixes. And, as it happened, today went well. I wasn't a bad dog mother after all. Russell walked for half a mile around the noted field. Jack walked with us once with his electric collar keeping him from running off. While Russell spent most of the sunny afternoon on a chain, tethered to keep him from blindly wandering into the busy road, or the creek bordering my parents' property, he did get the chance to wander, and frolic, eating bird seed much of the time. As for Ben Franklin, and this valiant transition? Detoxifying has its drawbacks, namely walking up late, later, and late. This is not good for Russell, but we're all trying to change.

# 1/10/16

I NEVER HAD CHILDREN. WHY? I WANTED PRACTICE. That, I've already made clear. Jack and Russell are both special needs, so I don't get to write in this journal as much as I should, or could. Rain ruined the prospect of any excitement over the past few days. I'm trying my hardest to keep up with Ben Franklin's schedule, but, being on an anti-psychotic, I can't seem to wake up at five o'clock in the morning. Instead, the average is between nine o'clock, and nearly noon. This is not good for Russell. He needs to eat and receive his insulin by five o'clock, and at five o'clock in the evening. His eyes are getting worse as a result of my inability to take care of him. But, each day, I try, setting my alarms for five, and, each morning, I fail to wake up on time. As a result, he has dense cataracts, and severe glaucoma. His left eye is losing pressure, strangely, so it's sinking inward. Russell's credit care is almost maxed out, so I can't afford to take him to the vet; his bills average around three hundred dollars a month, and I barely make ends meet. I plan to return to work in spite of my poor health, but this won't happen until a patient job opens up, a job that is suitable for my skills set. Instead of turning away from alcohol, I turned toward it. I lost a full year of potentially good health, and Jack and Russell were the ones who suffered as a result. Don't get me wrong, I'm not a total demon. We went for long walks around lakes, and farms, and villages, but I could have done better. They're good dogs. When I was working, before I quit my job to take care of them, and myself, I had a hard time keeping up with them. I'd wake up late, or would be too tired to walk. And, then, there was the bad situation. Well, you'll see. Things will get better.

# 1/13/16

AT NOW THIRTY-SIX YEARS OF AGE, I HAVE TO TACKLE MANY challenges that draw me away from being a better dog mother to Jack and Russell. Namely, I've decided to follow my Master's degree in English with a medical degree. Medical school is challenging. It takes time, energy, and emotions away from being a decent dog, or cat, mother. All of these things I have weighed. I don't know what to do with Russell to heal him, in spite of my existing medical knowledge. He walked a mile on Sunday, but refused to walk the following day. Yesterday, I didn't even try. Why? Community work, which I have to do to even get an interview with a medical school, took away time. Jack and Russell both take glucosamine now. I made sure to order Russell's insulin early, buying 2500 beef flavored flex chews at the same time. If it was a perfect world, I'd have the money for quarterly vet visits, and much needed teeth cleanings. I don't have enough money, however. And, with a return to work looming, I'm not sure of how I'll manage long hours away from home. Fortunately, due to debt, I live with my parents who can care for Jack and Russell while I work, and do pre-medical classes. I won't be rich, but it will be enough of a salary to pay for a dog sitter to help my now retired parents. Do I come across as being worried? I am.

# 1/16/16

Rain ruined yesterday. Russell, and Jack lounged inside while I got exercise at the local gym. Sometimes, I wonder why I gained so much weight. Government service is hard, but, for me, taking care of myself while being abused by the government was harder. Between intelligence work, and working for the government by engaging in civilian service, I had my fill, and, I can now say, I'm done. I have plans. Not only plans for Jack, Russell and me, but plan that involve finally having a family. The lake sounds nice, but without extra money, that dream won't be realized. I plan to work as a psychiatrist only now, taking pre-medical classes at a local community college. There are no jobs for an MA in English. I write, but that money goes to retirement accounts, and charity. Ultimately, I have decided to simply write, finish my sabbatical, and finish the science and math classes required for medical school. Jack and Russell will be happy. In a year, I plan on moving, leaving my parents' house for renting, yes, at the lake. Only two years of in-class studies are required down the road, the rest will be up here, in Morganton, away from any major city in North Carolina. Working for the state mental institution is my goal, my passion. Before

Jack and Russell, I loved psychiatry, and the possibility of really helping the mentally ill. Russell's fine. Two days in a row, he walked a mile. Tomorrow, it will be another mile walked. Even Jack is getting a mile in at a local trail. They've gone for rides, and had treats. I am hopeful that we'll make it to Shining Rock, where they can dance, and wiggle once more, one last time while standing on the top of a mountain.

# 1/20/16

THE FIRST SNOW OF THE SEASON FINALLY CAME, AND Russell and Jack are nestled indoors. Over the last two days, the winter chill kept them from walking, but Russell did go for what I call a 'pooh-pooh' walk around the field, urinating, and making his territory. Jack seems to be less spritely with the cold weather, so I have him time off from walking around the town trail. Marion has been a good place for them in their old age. So much so, that I almost forgot that they are both 14 this year.

# 1/25/16

JACK AND RUSSELL'S FIRST BIG SNOW OF THEIR LIVES CAME a few days ago, and is still lingering, even with warmer weather. Russell simply stood in the snow, and shivered, while Jack managed to roam through the nearly two feet of fluffy snow. Dad plowed through a section of the property, so that the dogs didn't have to freeze in knee deep snow. The tractor still ran in spite of the weather. My anxiety increased with being snow bound, but was relieved after I took Jack and Russell out in the sunny weather following the storm, and I managed to, dare I say, play, making a snow angel, and even running in the snow to visit the neighboring horse. Jack seemed to thoroughly enjoy himself, playing with the other dogs. His white coat looked yellow against the blankets of snow. I can't say that the dogs have been happier in recent years. Even with my depression, and their age, the last few days have been a reminder to live, love, and laugh. When the snow melts, hopefully Jack, Russell and me will be able to maintain a focus and the momentum to really live. And, by June, hopefully both dogs will be able to hike without seizures, or ailments; healthy again.

# 2/8/16

A LOT HAS HAPPENED SINCE THE SNOW, WELL, BLIZZARD of 2016. Russell's health has drastically improved. However, he is still challenging his fate of decent health (by June). I woke up at ten o'clock this morning, but Russell usually receives his insulin shit by eight o'clock, giving him the spunk in his step to walk a mile a day. Jack tries to follow, but runs into trouble with the invisible fence. I focus on Russell right now, but will return to caring for Jack by the spring. Jack has seizures still, choking him out, and causing him a great deal of pain. I have considered walking them together around the field, but Russell is rather slow, while Jack sprints ahead. The groomers don't seem to mind either of them, in spite of their elderly age. Russell's eyes are now unsightly, and Jack has several masses on his neck, and body. When I am able to afford better care for them, I will seek it out. With all of my financial responsibilities, I have to be careful with money, but not with love. I often regret not caring for them enough, too busy to pause for a short walk. I'm hoping that they will both survive another season, another year, even. One last time, we'll hike to Shining Rock, not Sam Knob, and, both companions, blind, or blinding will feel the cool air of the Blue Ridge Parkway.

# 2/11/16

WHILE I DOUBT THAT A SNOW STORM WILL HIT THE Foothills again, both Jack and Russell, and me have colds, just in time for the coming of warmer weather. This season has been chaotic weather-wise. Summer temperature, and the arrival of a strange blizzard convince everyone of global warming's existence. The dogs didn't seem to mind. Once I am well, I am determined to lock both Jack and Russell into a daily routine of one mile each, once around the field six times for Russell, and once around the local walking trail for Jack. We'll see how that pans out for both of them, and me.

# 2/19/16

I AM BACK TO BEING A BAD DOG MOTHER. LAZY WAKE-UP times, lack of movement, and forgetting the dogs are still living essentially. Never fear, I will return to the mile a day for both Jack and Russell, and plenty of rides. More than anything right now, Jack, and Russell need to go to the vet to get shots, having their teeth cleaned, for geriatric blood panels, and to get plenty of supplies for the next few months, supplies including special prescription dog food, and glucosamine chews. Will I go to the doctor, or dentist? No. Unfortunately, on this economy, a parent of any kind has to choose between this-or-that. No one can afford to take care of the health of a child, furry, or not, and themselves. I plan to go back to work this year, but I will only make minimum wage. At best, I'll make thirteen dollars an hour. This is still not enough to care for both the dogs, and myself. So, I drink health drinks, get in eight glass3es of water, and exercise. Right now, I do a specific regimen to keep my teeth, nose, and ears clear, a type of detox for your head, I guess. I still drink coffee, but that will change when I have the sleep apnea mask to wear at night. One additional positive is that the CPAP machine will help me sleep at night without choking out, and ready me for a decent wake-up time. Right now? It's still nine, ten, or worse. I go to sleep at a good hour, but the nightmares from PTSD, and sleep apnea impede any normal wake-up time. Jack and Russell don't seem to mind. They sleep, also, unless Russell has gotten into the other dogs' food again, and is suffering from high glucose in his blood, making him urinate three times an hour. For instance, one of the other dogs didn't eat all of her food, as always, so, last night, Russell decided that it was delicious, again, and pigged out following a long walk. Needless to say, he urinated on the bed, waking up at three in the morning to relive himself. My goal is to wake up at five, not three, but the dogs have their mornings occasionally. Sometimes, I feel the same level of stress as when they were puppies. In spite of advice to think about my options, I'm not willing to put them down, ever. So, life will be trying, but I would rather see them pass naturally, and without pain. So, it's back to being a good dog mother, and a good person.

# 2/24/16

EVEN THOUGH THE WEATHER IS WARMER, RAIN DETERS any thought of walking around the field, or local YMCA trail. Russell, still, is doing better than before. Jack? The same for Jack. I have given up on waking up early, earlier than seven o'clock. Between sleep apnea, nightmares, and insomnia, I just cannot swing it. However, I will be following the Founding Father, Ben Franklin's daily schedule. Routine is important for a diabetic dog, something Russell has not yet had. Too much vata? I don't know. If I can begin my day at eight o'clock, I have great faith that Russell, and Jack, will be completely happy, even with their 14 years of age.

# 3/27/16

JACK AND RUSSELL HAVE HAD AMPLE REST. WHILE I have been busy managing my way out of what I finally admitted is a bad time, the dogs have not had as much exercise as they should have. That will change. I am now willing to deal with the bad time. And, the dogs will walk, sniff, and play once more, just in time for better weather. June is approaching. While I have to train Jack and Russell for the rigors of hiking, I am hopeful that everything will be settled, and I can take them on their walks, and short hikes.

# 4/10/16

Jack, Russell and me went on a grand adventure today, hiking through the Biltmore Estate's gardens, and walking around the respective lake. While the exercise was much needed, Russell (and Jack) struggled with the nearly three mile venture into nature. Jack choked out on numerous occasions, and Russell simply did not want to walk after half of a mile. Jack finally got the message about pulling when he had a mild seizure at the lake. The fun started at the pet store, where I purchased Russell's special prescription diet dog food. Russell pooped right in the entryway, from excitement, so I cleaned it up with one of his doggie pooh bags. Jack was overly energetic in the store, but mainly went crazy on the hike. I would say that I have become the perfect caretaker, but I have not, I'm afraid. I still have to rip myself out of bed before ten o'clock, and I do not keep up with necessities, such as walks, routine, and the much needed purchases that keep both Jack and Russell healthy. Russell has been eating the other dogs' food for the last three days, and, my how it shows. His eyes are closed with goo oozing out of them, and he seemingly only wants to nap. Fortunately, I had the sense to take the day for them today, not indulge myself, or friends.

# 4/14/16

THE DOGS HAVE BOTH ENDURED A LOT OF EXERCISE recently. So much so, that rest is in order. I'll take them hiking today, but just for two miles. Russell cannot tolerate extensive hiking yet. The blindness has him scared in any situation that is new, or lesser known. Jack enjoys walking, but has seizures due to choking, and not getting in air. Both dogs go to the vet next week for an annual check-up. Hopefully, nothing insane will come from their blood panel. I don't know what I'd do if I got bad news. Either way, I think that the dogs will be fine.

# 4/18/16

TODAY WENT WELL. IN SPITE OF THE HEAT, JACK AND Russell both endured a day of walking. Jack hiked for three miles around the YMCA in Marion, and Russell walked for nearly two miles. Both Jack and Russell will have their annual check-up tomorrow morning. I do hope that I will get good news. Russell's eye is sinking, however, but I am sure that it can be saved. By June, both dogs should be able to endure a Wilderness hike one last time, giving them both a final farewell to youth, and the golden days. I'm also pleased to note that we are now rising early, just in time for insulin, and a decent breakfast.

# 4/26/16

JACK AND RUSSELL ARE DOING WELL. I AM NOT. YEARS OF depression, I resolved the symptoms of depression, but kept this pest called PTSD. I have to take the medicine, which causes me to sleep in. Russell has to eat by five, receive his insulin shot, and get eye drops for the glaucoma. Frankly, I'm not really sure of what to do. I sleep for twelve hours on this Zyprexa medicine, sometimes even longer. The dogs are loved, but I always feel that I can do more, that I have, and am, messing up. I'll take them for a hike this June, stand out on the top of Sam Knob, or Shining Rock, and even wag my tail. But, I will feel as though I've failed them, that I have made too many mistakes. I'll feel as though they have loved me only, that I haven't loved them enough through action.

# 5/1/16

I am pleased to report that Jack is mission-ready. Yesterday, we took a true two and a half mile hike up to see Catawba Falls just outside of Old Fort. He choked out several times, but with adequate pressure applied to his neck, he did not seize. Russell stayed home, and rested since he keeps finding the high fat food meant for the larger, younger dogs of the house. Hopefully, a good diet with gentle rehabilitation will improve his chances of making the hike this June. It will be slow, but sustained. I've never thought of myself as being a good dog mother, but, at 14 years of age, the dogs are facing their one last thrill—the open air of the Blue Ridge Parkway, and the Pisgah National Forest.

# 5/5/16

Jack and Russell were roused from their sleep to go walking today. We did two and a half miles, although, Russell did not seem to enjoy it until the end. Jack pranced along, and tried to speed up his lagging brother. Jack's liver must be improving, as he spends a great deal of time outside, on the farm, playing, and hunting. Russell's laziness comes from eating the other dogs' food, which elevates his blood sugar, and stresses his pancreas. All the same, he, and Jack, are doing well. I have cut back their food, as a final note, as all of us have somehow gained weight.

# 5/9/16

Unfortunately, I am back to being a bad dog mother. Drunk last night, I ignored Russell, and woke up at nearly noon today, giving Russell his insulin shot way too late. I have not exercised the dogs beyond minor walk, walks around the field, for instance. Tomorrow, I hope to return to a good schedule, and recover from a night of stupidity.

# 5/19/16

THE RAIN, SUMMER RAIN, SLOWED ALL OF US DOWN. JACK and Russell seem to be eager to walk again, as they are bound to the house, at the moment. Russell keeps bouncing again, running into walls due to a mix of energy, and blindness. Jack has gained weight, and insists upon wandering in, and out of rooms. The younger dogs lay around, but any sound is a reason to bark themselves into a frenzy. Over all, Jack and Russell are doing well. I am taking a nurse aide course to begin my career in medicine, which is soothing for all. I do make a point of returning home for a five minute lunch, just to say hello to Jack and Russell before going back to class. Overall, everyone is fine.

# 5/25/16

JUNE IS ALMOST HERE, AND, I MUST CONFESS THAT JACK is fully prepared for a lengthy hike, but Russell is not. His diabetes seems to be causing him pain, so after a half mile hike, he stagnates, and even refuses to walk. All the same, I will take him to Sam Knob, to the Wilderness area. Both dogs are in better health, however. Russell actually has bouts of energy, and Jack behaves as though he is five years younger. I've learned that Jack's seizures come from him choking out. I simply massage his airway now to prevent him from seizing. I'm amazed at the rebound in both of them, and look forward to our last adventure together, however blind, or not.

# 5/29/16

Jack and Russell enjoyed a great adventure yesterday, going to the vet to obtain Russell's insult, which had nearly run out, and going to the pet store for treats, and the standard tour of the retail outlet. A long ride also had, we ventured home from Asheville, missing a chance to walk around Lake Tomahawk, but, with Jack and Russell's bellies full, I suspect that they didn't mind. With the rain today, both dogs are napping, and enjoying random snacks in the form of scraps. Jack seems to be particularly enthusiastic about my return to eating meat.

# 7/17/16

I WAKE UP LATE, HARDLY WALK, AND SWITCHED THE dogs' food for a luxury brand that has too much fat. But, I'm trying. Russell walks half of a mile, and so does Jack. We're happy, but unhealthy. I'm fat, Jack's fat, and Russell always seems to be starving. I planes for a five mile hike in June that never happened. But, still, somehow, we're happy. I quit one government job to job shadow as a nurse aide, and the interview is tomorrow. Hopefully, extra income will equate to better care for both sons. Sons, yes, sons. I'll never have human children, so Jack and Russell are it. Still, even with joyful days, I feel like I've failed, feel like I'm the cause of poor health, not their aging. C'est la vie, I guess.

# 8/28/16

THE SUMMER IS ALMOST OVER, AND I HAVE NOT TAKEN Jack and Russell for their finally walk out into the place called the Wilderness. Russell's health is poor, and Jack's health is declining. This is partly due to the fact that I began a job in healthcare, ironically. They wake up on time, but the weekend are saturated with a potentially fatal combination for them: my alcohol abuse, and subsequent sleeping in. In other words, I've failed them. I've never seen Sam Knob, or Shining Rock in the fall, so that's the new goal. Basic veterinary care will improve both Jack and Russell's mood, and overall health. Right now, due to financial problems, I only provide insulin, eye drops, and special food. They need more. Both dogs need their teeth cleaned, supplements, a variety in regard to their special food, and treat, better bedding, and daily, lengthy walks. As to whether or not I'll add these items to their care, I don't know. I have my own health problems, namely schizophrenia, depression, and PTSD. Over the years, Jack, and Russell have battled the illnesses with me, sometimes with successes, sometimes with sadness, excessive sadness. This journey at the end of their years isn't just about keeping them healthy, it's about an apology.

I failed many time, in many ways, even striking them once. My emotions took over, and they were forgotten, finding primary care with their grandparents, my parents. Maybe this is about me, my reconciliation with them, a time of happiness void of the pain, and confusion caused by mental illness. I can't go back, but there's always a new beginning in today. Every seizure, or fall reminds me that there is so little time left. They were my children, and I failed. That brings me to a place of acceptance, and a place of forgetting; a time to provide care, and offer happiness. So, Sam Knob? This fall.

# 8/29/16

Rounding out the day, I purchased Russell's insulin, soft, and dry food. I considered putting it off, but decided to go ahead, and care for both Jack and Russell completely. My feeling of having failed, as noted, might subside with simple purchases, and a boost in effort. Although, my health is poor, so that fat tends to resonate with Jack and Russell's care. I went to great lengths to care for them when they were puppies, even replacing six hundred pounds worth of carpeting with no fuss. But, more happened. I have been severely sexually abused in the military, and feel into depression. Somedays, I could barely take care of myself back then, much less Jack and Russell. They went for the Sunday walk just yesterday, but the past still eights me down. I think that it is time for forgiving myself. Their final years are meant to be special, comfortable. Money will come, and go. I will simply have to continue to wear the same old outfits, and shoes, never change my purse, not cut my hair, and refuse to wear make-up. Russell's overall bill is five hundred dollars a month, and I'm a disabled veteran paying off debts. Jobs will come, and so will more money. I'm going to live, and try, for them.

They were always there, always loving. I can't think of any better way of saying thank you than to make their finally years brilliant, and calm. We moved to a farm to do just that.

# 10/20/16

Jack and Russell have been neglected. I meant to do this, or that for them. It hasn't been done. Our hiking trip never happened. Their health declined again. So has mine. In spite of my repeated failures with them, I'm determined to make this work, give them a happy final year (potentially), final hike, and, in turn, receive their forgiveness. I spent fourteen years loving them, but suffered from a depression that robbed them of wagging tails, and excessive happiness. Their feelings were expressed at times, through growls, nips, and a lot of naps. I tried, but could have done much more. I didn't abuse them, I just never let them know that I, too, could love them. Their grandparents raised them, for the most part, while their mother was depressed, in the bed. Somedays, I want to go back, but then there would be illness, an illness that has all but vanished. I can take care of them now, and do. No more depression, and, hopefully, no more of a bad time. I'm free to choose their care now. So, today, they both went for a walk, ate healthy snacks, and food, and enjoyed a hot fall day filled with marking their territory. I have to still try. Each day, I face the anxiety of not knowing. They're fourteen, almost fifteen, and another year might not come.

# 5/8/17

WHAT HAS BECOME OF SEVEN MONTHS? JACK AND RUSSELL are fifteen years of age now, their teeth have been cleaned, and masses have been removed. Unfortunately, financial stress caused by bad time's impact on my spending prevented me from taking them to get their booster shots, and geriatric panels, but that has all passed. They seem to enjoy life now, with daily romping around the farm, in a wide open field that lets them roam for even up to an hour. Russell seems to enjoy the evening wander the most, in spite of his blindness. His glaucoma has completely taken his sight, but he enjoys sprinting about while Jack still have enough sight to examine mole hills with the younger dogs. I still have depression, depression that prevented me from caring for Jack and Russell all of those years, forcing me to rely on my parents for help, but I know that the last years of their lives will be their best. It all wasn't so bad, in other words. They were born in England, travelled, always had access to veterinary care, and hiked just as much as I did. However, that didn't mean their final days would involve hiking, apparently. I had such big plans, the final grand hike out into the Wilderness in Pisgah National Forest just off of the Blue Ridge Parkway. But, they're now old, and maybe I was trying not to age myself. Jack has seizures on walks, and Russell is blind, so aches and pains, as well as the aforementioned, present hiking. I have to be mindful of them now, love them. They seemingly need more attention now than when they were young. Both dogs loved to bark, hunt, dig, and chase lizards, paying very little attention to their mother. In some ways, I think that their needy elder years come from God giving me one last chance. Instead of depression, I sank into drinking, and during that time, I'm honestly surprised that Jack and Russell didn't die. They went through the bad time, just as much as I did. And, frankly, I can never forgive myself. So, here's to one last chance, and what of making their elder years exceptional? I now know that they will be, even for myself.

# 5/10/17

Russell defecated on the bed. I thought of no other way of stating that fact. It was a first, and included a day of washing the linens. He woke up around two in the morning, upset, so I plopped him on the bed for comfort, and went back to sleep. Something went wrong, as diarrhea also came out of him. He was so tired that he didn't move. Obviously, he'll be going to the local vet as soon as they have an open appointment. I love both of my dogs, so an incident normally ignored by others sends me into a tizzy. I ordered his insulin well in advance, so that won't be another reason for an episode. Other than that fine event, the dogs are enjoying global warming with lots, and lots of summer spell naps.

# 8/27/17

Today, Russell was put to sleep. He died.

# 9/7/17

JACK, AND MYSELF, ARE DOING MUCH BETTER THAN LAST week. Russell's death was hard to take. He suffered greatly, seizing from the diabetes, and obviously in a lot of pain. The emergency vet hospital was the place where Russell wanted to die apparently. The room was soothing, not cold, and sterile. His passing was peaceful. He was sedated, and then humanely put to sleep, literally. I lost it, all the same, crying noisily. Jack became depressed immediately, refusing to eat, and just napping. In time, Jack will pass. However, my goal is to spread some of the ashes of Russell over the mountains at Shining Rock, with Jack hiking with me. He is fifteen years of age, however. So, the preparation for the hike has to happen, and soon. Jack had a bad liver, bad back, and poops out on me while we're walking around the YMCA. I purchased a softer harness, but he still behaves as though he's suffering. In some ways, I think that Russell becoming ill was what he wanted. He was carried around the last three years, like Jack was when he was young. Now, Jack is carried around again. He takes his medication, but I have lost hope of him living another year. He's peaceful, we cared for, and can still see, and sense some things. The hike will be a challenge, but something that will unite them both again when Jack passes. And, when I pass. I will have some ashes spread there, too. I love them both like children, without ever doubting the sanity of my thinking.

# 9/14/17

RUSSELL'S REMAINS ARE SITTING ON THE DRESSER NOW. Jack sleeps in my bed. I've done everything to comfort him. Bad weather made it so we wouldn't go for a walk, but now I see that Jack could live to eighteen, all the same. I invested so much care, and attention to Russell that I all but ignored Jack. Now, I get a second chance. All that I did wrong can be made right. I can even take Jack with me when I travel, something he'd probably enjoy. The horizon is so far away, and now I can make his life better, if only I remember to care for myself, too. For now, the days will revolve around Jack's naps. But, soon, we'll do the rare thing of hiking in his old age.

# 9/16/17

JACK HAS DIFFICULTY WALKING WITH HIS NEW HARNESS, which is padded, or he simply doesn't want to walk. I debated ending his daily walking routine, but I think that it's too soon to know as to whether or not he's finally succumbed to lazy days of naps, and urinating on the floor. Russell's last days were such, so I'm bracing myself for a very real possibility that Jack has finally met his last year on planet earth. I often wonder as to whether or not Russell has anyone to snuggle with in heaven, since he was the first of all three of us to go. Jack seems to articulate that he misses his brother through moans, and groans. "I miss Russell, too," I tell him. Someday, I'll come to terms with his passing, but, for now, I'm grieving still, and so is Jack.

# 9/17/16

FINALLY, JACK DID IT. HE WENT HIKING. WE STARTED
out with an easy trail only a mile long. At the end, Jack
looked at me as though I was being cruel, so we returned
home. I gave him a hearty supper, and, of course, he
awoke in the middle of the night wanting food, and
water. At two o'clock in the morning, we returned to
sleep. Lazy, I slept in. Jack didn't. He already seems to
be healthier. Only time will tell if he's going to improve
health-wise, or decline. I've decided to feed him only his
special diet food; the other brand is toxic for him. All the
same, we have to continue on, continue hiking, walking,
and, ultimately, living.

# 9/21/17

FOR THE LAST FEW DAYS, JACK HAS BEEN RESTING. AT first, I thought that he was still grieving. I've realized since my initial concern that I'm simply exhausting him with affection, and care. He's no longer a puppy, but, in my mind, he still has the same energy. Years ago, he could still go on major hikes, but, now, at fifteen, even a mile is undoable; causing problems. All the same, I'd still like to take him to Shining Rock, where we will sprinkle some of Russell's ashes. It's about a three mile trail, so I will be carrying him more than likely, but I feel that it's important for closure, for a last display of love for Russell (and, Jack).

# 9/26/17

JACK SEEMS TO BE NORMALIZING INTO WHAT IS HIS unique routine, which, of course, involves a lot of napping. We go on a walk every few days, as the treks seem to completely wear him out. I still wake up looking for Russell. Jack still looks at me as though he thinks that I'll tell him when Russell's coming home. Both of us are depressed. Both of us should rest, but I rather think that living is in ord3r now. Someday, Jack will pass, and, someday, I'll have to hike out to our favorite spot, and let go. But, as for now, I am still most certainly grieving while living.

# 9/28/17

FOR OVER TWO MILES, JACK HIKED. HE'S BEEN ILL FOR THE last few days, but it let me know that he's ready for a lengthy hike, during which time we'll spread some of Russell's ashes. He's happier, but the small cheeseburger upset his stomach. And, for some reason, I can't get him to eat his prescription diet dog food. All the same, Jack's mood has improved greatly. Someday, he won't wake up, but I'm trying to prevent a premature death due to the loss of Russell, and subsequent depression on my part. Our next big adventure is Bryson City, and a national forest. It's a level hiking trail, so Jack will be able to manage the hike. It will be a good thing for both of us, I think, but especially for Jack.

# 10/1/17

THE FINAL PART OF JACK'S LIFE, I KNOW, WILL BE PLEASANT, and laced with affection. No more hikes, but a lot of love, and longish walks. There are festivals to be seen, cities to tour, and road trips to take. Many days will be filled with treats, and trips to the pet stores. Jack no longer will eat his prescription diet kibble, so I have to decide what is more important, quality, or basic care? Either way, I've closed the chapter of our lives with Russell, and tomorrow will be a good dog day, wrought with no more sadness, and tears, but joy.

# CHAPTER FINALE

AT NIGHT, I SOMETIMES WAKE UP WITH A DEEP GRIEVING pain. Jack at my side, I still miss Russell. I miss his personality, his character, humor, even his gluttony. He ate too much. So did I. I would share fattening foods with both Jack, and Russell. Russell's final days were difficult. He was screaming during the night, seizing. I often think of ways that I could have changed the outcome. I still want him to be alive. I still want to coddle him. He was my first son, along with Jack, who is still living, but on the decline. Russell loved without question. He was adorable, and sincere, and nothing can bring him back. I have his ashes set on my dresser. Each night, I look at the wooden box. Each morning, I do the same. At times, I cry, hug Jack, or simply feel sorrow. Jack seems to be lost without his brother. I write in this book to deal with the pain, but everything reminds me of Russell's death—the farm, the chores, even Jack's prancing around the house. I feed Jack a luxury food brand now. I can afford anything for his care given that Russell is no longer with us. It's not uncommon for me to spend nearly a thousand dollars a month on Jack's care. With Russell, I had to budget. His monthly care was astronomical, and Jack was, frankly, ignored. I carried Russell almost everywhere, with Jack following. Russell was blind, and Jack was relatively healthy. Now, Jack is the one who is spoiled. I buy him anything that is recommended, and treats, feed him human food, and care for him by taking him for rides, and the occasional walk. He seems chipper, ready for another day. Toward the end, Russell wasn't chipper. He had lost his personality, and was lethargic. I knew that something was wrong. He would drink his own urine, eat anything, and whine about what seemed to be nothing. Then, the seizures came. It wasn't long after that when he gave up. I remember the last moment of his life, holding him in my arms, crying. He had be sedated, then he was put to sleep with the last shot going into the catheter. He went limp, and I nearly fainted. The vet took his body, collapsing on a soft dog bed back to the operating room. After the door closed, it was the last time that I saw Russel, then, lifeless. I continued to cry. I continued to criticize myself, regretting everything. I had gone through a bad time, and Russell suffered because of it. I overate initially, feeding Jack and Russell too much, too. Then, I drank. And, to compensate, I bought Jack and Russell rich dog food, and various, numerous treats. They were my sons, and everyone knew. They knew how to get at me, paralyze me. I'm still grieving, though no longer in Asheville, enduring a bad situation. I was hurting; so was Russell. With Jack alone now, I am a survivor who still has extreme guilt. My dogs were my life, and, in the apartment complex, they knew. If my weekend activity didn't include my dogs, I didn't do it. I loved my dogs, and not just in their youth. I tried adopting other animals, but they always ended up in foster care. Dogs, cats, bird, and fish, nothing derailed my love for my two jack russell terriers. All the same, Jack and Russell were always welcoming, always kind to the other animals. However, when they were young, they would get into epic fights with each other, even snapping at me trying to separate them. They were feisty, but so was I. It was a perfect match; a perfect family. So, in my deepest despair over Russell's passing, I find serenity, solace in remembering the past. I love Jack, of course, but our young hiking days are over, and I lament. I'm older, and have bad feet, and stiff joints, just like Jack, I suppose. When we all last hiked together, the trail was moderate, but difficult for us. My only regret is that Russell, on the last hike, merely heard the waterfall, and woods, rather than seeing the splendor of western North Carolina. The smell of the hike seemed to motivate him, however, and he trotted along faster than Jack, never falling behind. When Jack passes, I'll take both of them, their ashes to their final resting place, a shining rock off of a beaten path. So many days, we hiked into the wilderness. So many times, we almost lived there, staying overnight. So, they will find a home there, with me upon my passing, as well. And, that, will be the end of our story.

# 3/6/18

CALAMITY CAME OVER ME, APPARENTLY. IN OTHER words, I am drinking red wine. That wouldn't be so bad if the daily consumption didn't result in silent heart attacks. I spent a week without my gambit of medicines, also, which gave me some idea that I had to self-medicate. At best, mental illness is chaotic. At worst, it's deadly. I'm somewhere in between the two, for better, or worse. My finances, weight, and dark circles under my eyes indicate that I'm leaning toward detriment, and I don't know why. I can't pin down why I'm drinking. I have no earthy idea why I spend more money than I take in on disability insurance, compensation intended for basic living expenses, and savings. I don't know why I overeat either. In the common tongue, I'm a mess, and seemingly unaware of it through my daily action, and inaction. I've also spent a week out of group therapy, and only visited the hospital that I am supposed to be going to on a regular basis for a medication refill. I try to be religious, but often get sucked into a schizophrenic delusion centered on the book of Revelation; namely, my thinking that I am the so noted Bride, a false belief, clearly. Sometimes, I want to die, but I am in a process toward adoption, and the little stinkers need me to remain their mommy-to-be. Eventually, I'll be their mommy, I hope. Dietary changes helped some of my brain function, but I stopped exercising. I have it in my head that I'm supposed to go to the gym at five in the morning to meet well balanced people. My alarm goes off, but I never wake up. I'll try again tomorrow, but I'm sure that I'll fail. I'll try not drinking tomorrow, also, but will fail. The unending downward spiral will continue, and I'll bling, and be in nursing school. I have to keep trying. Jack needs me to be his mommy now.

# 12/3/18

Jack wear pants now, but he exhibits no sign of passing anytime soon. He's active, and even energetic at times, and I still adore him. I miss Russell, however. Sometimes, it simply overwhelms me, and I forget to hug Jack. I've calmed down about spoiling Jack with food. His total monthly care runs over three hundred dollars, which includes his soft, and dry food, his medicine, and specific treats that help with joint pain, or his the shininess of his coat. At present, Jack is sixteen, and will likely live another year. And, I'm happy, finally, and so is he.

# 3/21/18

JACK'S HEALTH HAS IMPROVED. HE'S EATING MORE, walking, and sleeping through the night. In fact, I think that his health surpasses my own. I'm even considering taking him to the Wilderness to hike. I'll take Russell's remains, too, of course, but not spread his ashes; simply carry them to his former, favorite hike. Jack does need to go to the vet, but his medicine was over two hundred dollars, and too hefty of a charge for me to realistically be able to cover an annual appointment, also. He's my son, and as I take him through another year of his life, I will not treat him as though he's already dead.

# 3/22/18

FINANCIAL TROUBLE KEEPS ME FROM SPOILING JACK. To compensate, I take him for walks, feed him human delights, like ham, and let him sleep on the bed. By morning, Jack has jumped down, and I find him in his kennel, pants wiggled out of, and urine on the puppy pad. His eyes are cloudy with white cataracts. I need to take him to the vet more often, but I went through an ordeal, and am now strangled by debt. Today, I have to purchase dog food that I can't afford. Jack will go with me, but not in the vet to prevent him from getting sick, something that he can't withstand. Beforehand, we'll go for our daily mile-long walk. Afterward, I might give Jack more treats. He struggles with the walking path, however, which has numerous inclines. All the same, Jack makes it around, and it's a good finish for the day. I often get told that I treat Jack like a son. My thinking is: why not?

# 3/26/18

JACK'S EYE IS GIVING HIS PROBLEMS, AND HE'S DUE FOR HIS annual. Two birds with one stone. I've noticed the same pattern between Jack's eyes and Russell's eyes. Hopefully, he's not diabetic. Hopefully, he's okay, but I always have to be prepared. I always have to have enough money for the potential that I will have to bring Jack to the emergency veterinary hospital in Asheville. Jack isn't depressed, however. Nor am I. We walk daily, but didn't today. Usually, it's a mile, but Jack obviously can't see. He's bumping into things, and me. Hopefully, it isn't bad news. I have to keep hoping.

# 4/4/18

JACK WHINES CONSTANTLY, NOW, FOR HUMAN DELIGHTS like turkey, or hamburger. I spoil him, but have no regrets. Tomorrow, he gets his teeth cleaned. He went to the vet recently, and was given a clean bill of health. I miss Russell still, at times, but try to make due. Jack needs me now. He seems to be scared of death, and I'm not sure that he really understand what happened to Russell. Jack does wander through the house routinely, as if he's lost without his brother. I know that I am lost without Russell. Days have become months, and I seem to think that Jack will live forever.

# 4/21/18

JACK OCCASIONALLY FROLICS, DANCES, AND EVEN attempts to jump. It reminds me of Russell when he was young. Days go by, and I wonder when Jack might pass. He's sixteen, after all, and does receive veterinary care, but has serious health problems. I look at him like he's a puppy still, and, sometimes, I get deep pangs of pain when I remember Russell. Both dogs have had a good life. Both dogs will never be forgotten. I'm writing in this journal to recall the good times. When the bad time came, there were, well, bad times. Because of that, Jack is now spoiled.

# 5/7/18

JACK HAS BECOME A PROFESSIONAL NAPPER. HIS DAILY exercise is mainly just running around on the farm. A walk around the YMCA became too much for him, so he spends most days at home. However, on occasion, I take Jack for an outing, such as a short hike, or a brief walk by the river, which he still enjoys, although he is slow, and exhausted by the end of the walk. I entertained the idea of going back out to Shining Rock, and spreading Russell's ashes, but, the last time we went, Jack didn't make it. Rather, I think that I will simply wait until Jack passes, and spread both brothers' ashes together.

# CHAPTER FINALE DEUX

AT SUNSET, I ENTERED MY TWO BEDROOM APARTMENT east of Asheville. Jack and Russell came to the door, wagging their tails.

"Hey, sweet peas," I said. "Mommy works now."

With a damning diagnosis, I thought that I'd never work again, but I landed a job as a billing clerk for medical insurance. I didn't necessarily like the job, but I needed the money. Making little over a though dollars a month, I was still heavily relying on disability income. The first week, I had no one to look after Jack and Russell. On my first payday, I hired a dog sitter.

"Hello, my name is Rebecca Pace, and I was wondering if you would be available to dog sit two geriatric dogs in an apartment setting?"

"Sure. Now, the first thing that I do is meet with the animals to make sure we're a good match. When could you do the first meeting?"

"I work during the week, but I could meet in the evening."

"That'd be great. How about five tomorrow?"

"Five tomorrow sounds good. I'll see you then."

The dog sitter sounded like a dream. She was

affordable, and flexible. But, I'd rarely been separated from Jack and Russell. In Durham, I lived close enough to work to do my own dog sitting. They needed me, and I needed them. In Asheville, there were no apartments close to work, so I had no choice but to hire a professional dog sitter.

"Okay, so it's twenty-five dollars for one pet per day."

"So, that's eight hundred dollars a month?"

"Yes."

"Okay, that's fine. Frankly, I have no choice."

"I understand."

The bill was steep, but the sitter was going to let me break it into two payments, which I could afford. Anything she requested, I obliged—new harnesses, better leashes, anything. Everything was going well until I encountered discrimination in the work place. An employee went into my medical record, and told all of the other employees that I had schizophrenia. I became depressed. The depression lasted a week, then a month, then I was no longer able to function. I was almost late every day, leaving Jack, and Russell unfed until the sitter came some days, and they were backed up on occasion, too. The sitter became their primary caretaker. I was becoming suicidal, so I took time off, nearly a month. During that time, I was a perfect dog mother again. I had a decision to make, however. I was being brutally harassed, threatened at work, so, one afternoon, I handed in my badge, and left the job site for good. Jack and Russell slowly came back around to better health. I loved them too much to give them up, so, I went shopping, almost daily, for them. I took out credit cards, and burned through savings. Something else was going on, not just my love for my dogs; namely, the bad episode.

I was a disabled veteran. No one believed me, and I was getting sicker. By November of 2014, I was buying cases of beer, and trying to drink them, even while taking my psychiatric medications, and having to still care for my two dogs. By 2015, I was an alcoholic, living each day to drink, and love my sense of sensibility. Jack, and Russell were neglected, and I had to Russell to the vet. I had credit, but no money. Emergency pet care ran into the thousands, but my guilt was telling me not to care.

"Okay, so I'll send over the paperwork, and they'll be waiting for him," the vet said.

"Okay, Mr. Russell, you're going to see the doctor."

The hospital was thirty minutes away. I also took Jack. Russell was lethargic, and sleepy. Jack was panting with excitement. It was not yet time to put Russell down.

"Hi, I have Russell."

"The diabetic?"

"Yes."

"Okay, I need you to fill out this form, and then have a seat in the waiting area until you're called back to one of our examination rooms."

"Okay, thank you."

My nerves calmed when the vet tech was teaching me how to care for my little diabetic. I feared for the worst, but the staff assured me that it was common in dogs, and that Russell's case was no unique.

The bill for specialized treatment ran into the thousands for overnight care. I wanted Russell to live, to give him another chance at geriatric happiness after a year of his mother simply not being able to function. Within a week, Russell had perked up, and was able to frolic again. I stopped drinking. The insulin had to be administered twice a day, with twelve hours spacing out the injections. I had to wake up early, but felt saved by my furry son.

Weeks into Russell's care, I saw a drastic improvement in both Russell and Jack's health. But, my own was slowly evading daily life. Soon after, I was worse, diving deeper into binge drinking. I still cared for Jack and Russell, but they engaging in minimal activity, even though I spend thousands on their care, taking them to the vet for any minor illness, even kennel cough. I was soon drained financially, borrowing more, and more, and, in time, an intervention happened, and I moved in with my parents, on their farm. The dogs were happy again. They could roam five acres, and I sobered up. So, we once again went for daily walks, even short hikes.

# 5/23/18

JACK WENT TO THE VET AGAIN, THIS TIME FOR HIS URINE screening that will tell if he has a tumor in his bladder, then, also for his seizures. Last night was bad. He seized, on, and off, for eight hours. I could hear the gossip. I am part of an animal right organization now, so I'm not putting him down. He's my son, and so was Russell. Jack will live out his days. I'm determined to allow his that chance, just like Russell had. If he has a tumor, I just have to give him even more medicine. That's all. In time, he'll decline, but he still has spunk in his step.

# TOMS CREEK

RUSSELL WAS ALWAYS THE PULLER. SO, ON HIS LAST HIKE, he pulled. Ahead of Jack, he clawed to get in the lead. And, get ahead he did, just to a spot to mark territory. Jack did the same.

At the trailhead, the hike was flat, with a clear path. This was necessary, because Russell was blind. In spite of his blindness, he scurried on, wandering to the left, and, then, to the right. Eventually, hikers approached, so I pulled both dogs back, and kept them close. We dredge through a water way, and a bridge, built recently. At the end of the bridge, there was an ascent. Russell went to the side, so I pulled him back, guiding him to the first stopping point. I was overweight, and had poor cardiovascular health, so we stopped a half a mile in, and then at another half mile mark, at the top. The view was something that we had taken in before, but when Russell was able to see. A waterfall drowned out all of the noise, and Russell was listening to the peaceful cascade. It was time to go home.

We turned around, and headed to the car. I could see Jack and Russell both smiling again, and had no idea that, within months, Russell would die. Jack still lives now, almost eight months after Russell's passing. And, sometimes, I think that he'll live for another two years. However, that isn't likely. He'll die, too, and I'll have to keep living.

# 5/29/18

JACK HAS EVEN MORE COMPLICATIONS GOING ON. Now, he has a tumor in his bladder, supposedly. I'm having to administer a higher dose of his seizure medicine, also. After the vet confirms that the blood in his urine is from the tumor, he'll take even more medicine. I spend at least five hundred dollars a month on his care, money that is, at present, borrowed. Almost out of debt, I had to start borrowing again to pay bills. I can't put Jack to sleep. He'll still spunky, and living a quality of life that is better than expected for his being sixteen years of age. He's even able to go for a mile long walk. Sometimes, I fear that he won't wake up. He seizes at night, but always makes it to dawn.

# 6/27/18

THE VET SENT JACK'S URINE TO THE LAB, BUT THE SAMPLE was compromised. Today, that will be one duty—getting a sample of urine. Supposedly, the tumor in Jack's bladder is bleeding, so he has urine in his blood. Sometimes, I want to move out of my parents' house, but with Jack's bills, I simply cannot. We live on a farm, anyhow. I'm not sure of how much longer Jack has. He'd elderly, but able. I'm tired though. Russell was hard to let go of, but I like I'm ready to let go of Jack, which isn't fair for him. I have the perfect job, writing, but no energy. As the dogs aged, I gained weight, too. So, as it stand, both Jack, and I are overweight, thus, lethargic.

# 7/2/18

JACK REFUSES TO SLEEP AT NIGHT. I HAVE BEEN GOING TO bed early, but Jack insists on urinating on the bed, or floor if I do not wake up, and take him outside. This has been going on for almost a year. When Russell died, Jack seemingly lost it. He began doing senile things, like scratching on an already open door, thinking that I was calling him, and drinking his own urine. The vet has given him medicine, but he often simply refuses to take it. I wrap the pills in meat, and, somehow, he manages to spit the pill back out. I cover the pill with peanut butter, and he licks around it, leaving the pill in the bowl. It's frustrating. Jack seemingly wants to die, but I don't want him to.

# 7/9/18

IN A MONTH'S TIME, I'VE FAILED TO GET THE REQUESTED urine sample to the vet. Part of me wonders if that failure is driven by fear, doubt, or just laziness. Jack still urinates blood, but he seems to be in good spirits. His bill is still astronomical, but comforting him with luxury food, and all of his needed medicine is something that I simply won't compromise. I considered taking him for a final hike, but his joints seem to bother him. All the same, I might drive out to the Parkway, and find a final resting place for his to enjoy in the afterlife, bringing Russell's ashes, too.

# 7/27/18

JACK IS NOW DECEASED.

# CHAPTER FINALE
# DEUX, ENCORE

JACK AND RUSSELL ARE BOTH DEAD. AFTER FIFTEEN, AND sixteen years of age, they both passed out of life into death. And, honestly, I felt like committing suicide. They were my sons. And, they both became extremely ill. Jack had cancer, stopped eating, and was going into a state of delirium before his final days. He was a fighter, but couldn't fight off all of his illnesses. Even at the end, he tried to fight, seizing, and screaming while dying. Russell died the same way, basically. Now, they are both together. I still have to hike out to Shining Rock, and spread their ashes. I still have to let go. But, I don't want to just yet. I lost my appetite, stopped exercising, and felt like overdosing on my psych meds. I cry almost constantly. When I lost my grandparents, and my aunt, it wasn't this bad. I'm crying now, as I'm writing this. All I can think about is when they were young, happy, and hopping through the field out at Sam Knob's basin. They looked like little deer, and loved the grass, and flowers. They were my sons, for God's sake. I was young, twenty-two, and decided to have them instead of children. Just yesterday, I lost Jack, ending my life with Jack and Russell.

I'm still crying. I'm having to force myself to eat, and not drink alcohol. All of the emotions of loss are mixed with a feeling of love, the deep love that a parent gives a child. Jack's passing seemed to happen last Monday, when a kitten was found in a tree by the road. Someone threw the kitten out of a car window while driving by, and Jack's health dove after I was left with no choice but to adopt the kitten. Jack was always good with cats, so he didn't seem to mind taking care of the kitten. Then, he stopped eating, drank water all of the time, and started urinating all over the place. Clearly, he was ready. I wasn't. It took a week before I realized that he was ready to die. The only thing I regret is not letting go. Jack was scared at the vet, and had to be sedated. He seized right before he died, but passed without pain. I often think of things that I did wrong. I was too hard on Jack and Russell in 2004. They kept digging where I was renting, and I had to spank them. They went through everything with me, that's what I mostly regret. In 2002, I was still going through military sexual trauma. So, they did, too. I would often come home, and cry. I lost my grandmother, and adopted them, so they initially went through grief with me. There were military men who would break into my house after I left the Air Force. God only know what the dogs went through. I tried to spoil them. I spent too much, I suppose, buying them presents to deal with pain when I should have been saving for retirement. But, that's how it should be. Jack and Russell had good lives in spite of the trauma. I became mentally ill, and was more detached, but I always put them first, through poverty, and through the abuse that I endured. I loved them, and they loved me. That's all that I want the world to know.

# PART THREE

It has been months now since Jack passed. And, with raising a new kitten, all that I can think about is how he reminds me of Russell, and how I need to adopt another kitten who reminds me of Jack. There's no meaning to life without the enduring friendship of dogs, or cats. And, after Jack's passing, a year nearly after Russell's death, I almost failed as a kitten mother, drinking so much that the kitten attacked me routinely, presumably trying to remind me to live, and live without regret. To me, the regret was overwhelming. I wasn't always a perfect dog mother. Now, I'm sober, so the kitten is fine, without agitation, but I still have those deep feelings related to loss likened to the loss of children. I look at the kitten now, and find joy. Initially, that wasn't the case. To start, I was angry, almost blaming the kitten for Jack's letting go. Philippe, the kitten, seemed to sense my feelings, something that I could gather by his biting, and scratching. When Jack first saw him, he seemed to sigh, as if he felt that he could finally pass. I was tired, too, and Jack probably knew that. The pampers, the pills, the special meals that I couldn't get him to eat, the financial stress, all of it came to a head, and I walked into the living room, and told my parents that I was going to put Jack to sleep. After all, he had cancer. And, there were numerous other illnesses at play. I just simply couldn't take it anymore. He had been dying. And, I was pissed off. Russell's passing was over-the-top with howling, and even screaming. I didn't want Jack to go through the same type of end to his life. I wanted him to choose. And, he did. Following the Monday phone call from the vet, by Thursday, Jack refused to eat. He wouldn't even eat meat cooked for him. He looked anorexic, and old, and it was evident that joy had left his life. He didn't wag his tail. He stopped wiggling. He even stopped greeting me. I knew, but didn't want to accept his passing, too. I wanted a good sign that he was ready. Oddly, I could hear him utter what sounded like, "I'm ready to go." Dogs can't speak, but jack russell terriers can. They're very intelligent, and often sound as though they're talking, speaking as their owners do. So, it was either Jack, or my sadness. Either way, we went to the specialized animal hospital where Russell died on that July day. Jack was carried in. The admin made me put him on the ground. Something happened. He danced, and wagged his tail. I didn't know what to do. Suddenly, he was happy, and I didn't know why. As if he was trying to be the perfect son right up to the end of his life. I looked down, ashamed. I had failed. I had really failed. I let a bad time rip apart my life, and lost four years of time with my sons, Jack and Russell. I'm better now. I have Philippe. The assailants have been restrained. But, they still break the protective orders. However, I refuse to let them trap me in a web of degradation. I'm headed to nursing school, have another job waiting for me, I'm almost out of debt, and things are better. But, that moment when Jack danced haunts me. It still leaves me with an overwhelming sense of loss. I have to be grateful, however. Jack left me with Philippe. When I first adopted Jack, and Russell, I was saved, rescued from a lonely, difficult life. Philippe save me from despair. And, I think that Jack knew that, and did let go. I will never know why he danced, pranced, and wagged, but I will always remember what the vet tech said: "This dog has been through everything medically." I felt like I had failed. At the same time, I knew that it was time for Jack to pass, even though he was a fighter. He didn't want to die. That's the reality that I had to deal with. I didn't cry until I reached the parking lot. He was my son. And, I had lost a child, yet again. I had a connection to Jack, and Russell that I don't have with Philippe, admittedly. Cats are different, and Philippe know that he's not a dog, Jack, or, Russell. So, he bites, presumably trying to remind me to love him, too. I'm also adopting human children. It's a strange feeling, such a deep sense of loss, such a deep love, missing them every day. So, I lost Jack, and Russell, but will gain a new life, filled with love, and lots of chocolate milk, and cheese puffs, and, of course, cat treats. Philippe won't tolerate my sadness. He lets me know that I should move on, get it together, write, attend nursing, and all of the rest. But, there are times when I want to go back, fix things that went wrong. Writing is therapy. Every time that I want to go back, to feel the joy of having Jack, and Russell in my life, I write. The first book that I wrote was a memoir about military sexual trauma that I wrote in graduate school when Jack and Russell, and me, were living on the side of a mountain.

They enjoyed life there, in Cullowhee, North Carolina. But, looking back, I should have written about my life through their eyes. It would have been more telling, albeit fiction. When my grandmother died, I cried like a groaning child for hours. So much so that Jack and Russell, then puppies, cuddled up together, and whimpered. They were my sons. My sons. I lost a baby after being raped, and adopted them. I wouldn't change a thing, but, in some ways, I wanted the baby, too. It was one of the darkest times of my life. I survived it, but was numb. I had been raped as a child, also, more than once. Then, in the Air Force, it was a routine experience. The only light in my life was the day that I decided to adopt two dogs, and of the same gender. I went on the LAN, and found a listing for jack russell terriers. The puppies were the only options listed. The caretakers wanted one hundred pounds for two. I couldn't refuse. I ended up with two boys instead of two girls, but I wouldn't anything for the world. With the boy puppies, I was finally free, finally able to have real fun. The first day Jack and Russell went for a walk, they wanted to go again. Jack went to the door, and would point with his nose to the leashes. There were beautiful moments. I took extraordinarily good care of both dogs. Everything was fine. Then, I was raped again. And, as such, I became depressed, and mentally ill. Illness, or course, had been budding anyhow. I couldn't control emotions anymore, and, over time, I was unable to function. So, the dogs went to Zebulon, North Carolina, to my family, and to a house where the only threat was them getting fat. (And, they did.) The time I spent in England alone was difficult. I tried to kill myself. I got into a major car accident. And, I still kept trying to survive rape. In the end, I bunkered down, knowing no one, and spending the weekends alone, going to see London plays, and consuming a bottle of wine at night. The dogs were enjoying their new home, barking, and digging, chasing squirrels, and befriending other dogs. Jack's favorite activity was killing garden snakes. Russell loved hiding bones. My parents, at the time, were obese, so they didn't walk Jack and Russell, but, when I finally made it home, Jack and Russell went on daily walks around the neighborhood, and to the park. They especially enjoyed trips to pet stores, and rides of any kind. By far, the most exciting time for Jack, and Russell was Christmas. I would buy everything from bones to biscuits, and they loved it, wagging, barking, and even jumping on Christmas morning. I'm trying to resume the tradition with Philippe. This Christmas, in 2018, will be his first morning of joy. Jack and Russell didn't have a Christmas until they were nearly two. As I write this, my pain dissipates. As I read what I have written, it returns. They only thing in my life, right now, that relieves the feeling of loss, is Philippe. In the future, it will be kids. In the very near future, in fact. Part of me wonders whether or not I'll be a good mother to my future children. I know that I'll try. I'll look back on Jack and Russell's lives with great joy, but with great remorse. I went through a lot, and so did they. I live with my parents now, so I am safe. I don't make myself particularly susceptible to abuse anymore, as though I had been groomed to endure it. I just regret that Jack and Russell are not here to experience a better life. I no longer want a partner. That's been part of the feelings of new joy. By just having a family, I know that Philippe will be happy, showered with love. I'm often too hard on myself, of course. But, the reality is that both Jack, and Russell became very ill. I fed them too much, spoiled them with treats. The vet kept emphasizing a healthy weight for both dogs. I didn't care. I was morbidly obese myself, and so, the dogs were, too. I'm at a healthier weight now, but I still overeat. It has to stop. When you adopt children, you have to nearly be perfect—no debt, healthy eating habits, and well balanced in all ways. I wish that I had read books about Jack Russell Terriers like I read parenting books. They would have been happier. I never could figure out why they would bark so much. Anytime that I would leave, they'd howl in a chorus. Anytime that I'd sit outside, they'd bark, and get into vicious fights. In some ways, I didn't understand them. In other ways, I was a perfect mother, letting them sleep on the bed, feeding them premier food, taking them on long hiking trips without a leash, and so forth. In spite of this, I was numb, cold even, from mental illness. Jack would drink river water, then urinate right in front of me, on the rental's carpet flooring. Russell would try to attack neighbors. Every day was a struggle. To understand my failings fully, I have to go back to the beginning, back to 2002 on RAF Lakenheath. I shouldn't do this unsurprised. Usually, going back in writing, to a time of major trauma without a psychologist leads to a psychotic break, as I learned in 2006, when I wrote the bulk of a memoir about military sexual trauma. But, there is no way anything can be retold, revisited without it having already been described in the former memoir. So, here it goes, a retelling while including the bravest, most valiant of dogs, Jack, and Russell.

# PART FOUR

SOME MAY VIEW A RETELLING OF AN ALREADY RETOLD story as being redundant, or even vain. I don't. Rather, I think that a revisiting of the already noted memoir in the first part of this book will lead to truth reborn, and probably a more accurate overall story. So, instead of revision, the reader gets a rehashing. So, I'll begin at the beginning, when I was sitting at my desk, looking at a computer owned by the government, on the LAN, clicking on the animal exchange category, and seeing that there was only one siting. The listing was for jack russell terriers. I made the phone call, and agreed to the one hundred pounds for both male dogs, puppies who would arrive without any vaccinations, and long tails. I didn't care. I loved them the minute that I saw them. Russell was predominately brown, while Jack was mainly white. Both were tri-color dogs. I went directly from the military personnel flight to RAF Mildenhall, taking to, and soothing the two new puppies with a local classical music station that was playing Mozart. We got to the other nearby base, and I took their cage to the entry way of the Base Exchange. Not able to take them into the store, I nearly left them I the front when a nice family offered to watch them. Saved, for the time, I went into the store, and immediately purchased everything from food to bedding to toys. After only ten minutes, I left RAF Mildenhall, and the puppies continued to sleep to yet another classical symphony. I wasn't sure of how the overseer would receive the news of puppies. I had received permission to adopt dogs, but not jack russell terriers. He wasn't he. But, his skepticism calmed when I assured him that I would take excellent care of them. And, I did. However, long days at work let to even bigger messes at home. Carpet was pulled up, newspapers ripped to shreds. Nothing worked to deter the little ones from being destructive. So, I started to walk the puppies in the evening. They loved it. Jack was especially fond of the lengthy trail around the neighborhood. Russell, however, was fearful of cars zooming by. He'd claw at my arms, terrified. Jack was an A student. Russell always had to be difficult. When Russell became diabetic, I almost laughed. He had, since being a puppy, always needed more attention. The pictures that I took tell the story more so than me telling the story on the page. We didn't have a lot of money, but Jack and Russell's bellies were always full, making them rather round. They refused to sleep in the bathroom, so they slept on my bed with their little heads resting on my pillow. With a twin bed, I could hardly move, but being uncomfortable was worth getting sleep (no howling). It was as though everything was perfect, then something happened—my grandmother passed away from cancer. The puppies knew that something had gone wrong, really wrong. I would go through severe bouts of depression, crying endlessly. One time, I scared them with my wailing. It was a difficult time. A week later, I went to the animal boarding resort, dropped off the puppies, and went to the University of Cambridge for a summer study session, taking leave to go do what my grandmother thought would be a life changer. So, I went. I got to Cambridge, and within a week, I was at the boarding resort visiting Jack, and Russell. I wasn't speaking to anyone, as though I had gone mute. I confused everyone around me. Why was I so quiet? Jack and Russell soothed me. I felt their speaking with each wiggle. Back at Cambridge, the lessons had become more challenging. I didn't visit the puppies again. Instead, I read every book that I could buy. I soon became knowledgeable of both the British Raj, and Ancient Greece. Without Jack and Russell, however, for more than two weeks, I ran up to a small village near Bury St. Edmunds, and picked them up from their holiday—a large boarding area filled with attention, treats, and an open, but closed running area. I knew picking them up, that they were my sons, that I would be challenged, and that I couldn't give up on them, no matter how many things they tore up. When the escapes into the neighborhood started to happen, and the overseer had had enough—before he articulated that fact—I made the phone call to my mother, and father, asking if I could send Jack, and Russell home to Zebulon, North Carolina. They agreed, and over the pond came my mother to my Bury St. Edmunds flat. The overseer was relieved. Before the dogs left, I was in tears, wanting them to stay, and partly because I didn't want to live in England anymore. I had put in my separation request in July, and had been denied release. So, I applied again. And, once more, I was denied. It took a full year to get home. Even leave wasn't granted.

The war was on, and no one got out. But, in May of 2003, I saw Jack and Russell again. This time, in Zebulon, North Carolina, where I had grown up. The puppies had grown. No longer small butterballs that I gave birth to, they were wild, wiggly little dogs, excited, seemingly, by everything. Jack, for instance, saw me, and did a four feet jump, and wiggle. Russell still went to the food. There were other dogs at home, also. A boxer, and miniature pincher, respectively. Jack and Russell loved the mini-pin. When she was attacked by a neighborhood dog, they both barked to the rescue. She lost her leg, but not her life. The boxer was the alpha dog, and he wanted both Jack and Russell to know it, especially when he picked Russell up in his mouth. He would attack them, but that never seemed to stop them from challenging him. Overall, Jack and Russell enjoy living in Zebulon, but our time was broken up by stints in Sylva, Cullowhee, and Durham, and a failed attempt at getting them to accompany me while I was teaching English as a foreign language in South Korea. The start of dog travel was Sylva, North Carolina, down the road from Western Carolina University. Most days were pleasant—walks alongside the Tuckaseegee River, meditating on rocks, chasing blue herons, a happy life. But, no day went by without Jack and Russell getting into fights, seemingly from frustration, or boredom. After all, we were in an apartment, and not on the first level, which made getting to their bathroom difficult. I learned quickly that river water was especially potent, as Jack would urinate repeatedly after going down to the river. Sometimes, he would urinate right in front of me, looking at me with disdain. Over time, I learned how to read his silent ques, and how to keep Jack and Russell from fighting, as well. I made mistakes, admittedly. Once, when Russell charged a neighbor, I pulled back on his leash so quickly that he rolled back, and hit his head on the bottom stair of the duplex. I was mortified, and so was my neighbor. Then again, with bad behavior (namely, barking), I simply started screaming at Jack and Russell, only making matters worse. With Philippe now, I'm careful not to repeat mistakes. After all, I'm older now, and read his ques, still not understanding all of them, admittedly. When I got another puppy, company for Jack and Russell, it was time to move. Jack and Russell didn't receive the puppy well, in the same way that they thought that two adopted kittens were squeaky toys. All the same, I kept her, and named her Lily. We moved to a house with a fenced yard. It was much easier managing three dogs with a fence, but I still took the dogs hiking, and let them run wild (we were in the woods). It, still, wasn't completely easy. Jack and Russell finally calmed down, but Lily was a hound mix, and she let me know it. The boxer loved her, but Jack felt dejected, and mostly looked depressed. Needless to say, a year later, I surrendered Lily to the animal shelter. I had become mentally ill, and wasn't able to care for three dogs. Jack's mood lifted after Lily found a new home. However, still to this day, I regret giving her up. I often wonder about whether or not she had a good life. After making that mistake, I was sure not to make another. So, even with becoming mentally ill, Jack, Russell and me moved to Asheville, North Carolina from the deep heart of the mountains. It wasn't even a year before I moved home, however. Later, I received a diagnosis:

paranoid schizophrenia. The dogs would suffer, too. I was disabled, shell shocked, and unable to readily communicate. For three years, Jack and Russell went through my illness with me. I also had PTSD, and depression. Even when I tried to work, moved to Durham, it was an awful experience for both myself, and the dogs. I was poor, and ill. The dogs became overweight, seemingly soothing themselves with food. I cried routinely, refusing their affection. I made the decision to go to South Korea in the middle of a delusion. The dogs were with my parents for five months. Jack ran toward I-40 looking for me. Russell was reportedly depressed. I came home, but came home worse off than I was before. I experience so much anxiety that I couldn't walk, sometimes couldn't even breathe. The boxer, Jack and Russell, and the mini-pin all put their ears down the first time that I almost went to the emergency room. No doctor could figure out what was wrong, so I went on a slew of anti-psychotics, and had an allergic reaction to one, leading to another episode. With plenty of time to relax, Jack, and Russell became obese while I maintained a healthy weight. Eventually, I was able to walk again, and walk the dogs. They rested with me for months, so they were excited to start working out again.

---

Overstricken with grief now, it's hard for me to return to when Jack and Russell were alive. I now have Philippe, but only complex feelings emerge. I want Jack and Russell to be alive, and to have Philippe. Too late, I wake up often in the middle of the night. Both dogs would need to go out, so, around one in the morning, or three, I wake up thinking that they're on the bed when it's really only the kitten. Grieving, I return to sleep, resting until Philippe awakens, usually around six o'clock in the morning. His cry makes me forget them. But, many time throughout the day, I weep, mourning their loss still. I sometimes consider adopting a puppy, but the kitten wouldn't tolerate one, so I change out the litter box, prepare fancy meals, and pet Philippe. This is my new life—caring for the cat.

———————————

Mental illness not only took away my sanity, but it also took away my ability to care for Jack and Russell. Reliant on my parents, we lived at home until I tried living in an apartment—a mistake. I was paranoid, and full of anxiety. We spent most of our time with my parents. I didn't work, and, then, I got a temporary recession job working at the Veteran Affairs hospital in Albuquerque, New Mexico. I couldn't believe it, and Jack and Russell were excited to go somewhere, and hopefully have a happy mother. Along the journey out to the great America Southwest, I forgot to take my medicine, so I was nearly manic, talking to the dogs, and imaging that someone was actually listening. It was pure joy. We stayed in roadside hotels that allowed pets. Jack and Russell seemed happy enough, and, though exhausted, I was, too. We didn't go very far into the surroundings of I-40, however. Our time was limited, so Jack and Russell simply had new places to sniff outside of the hotels. In three days, we were in New Mexico, with a surprise. The hotel was aged, and in a hostile side of Albuquerque. Jack and Russell had to nap while I was at work. It was a disaster. I couldn't wait until we found an apartment. Then, there was endless shopping for items needed to set up our lives in our new home. I was failing as a dog mother. I had no money, but I bought countless toys for the dogs. Jack and Russell were still neglected during the day. I spent ten hours away from home. They were depressed. Eventually, I quit, and called home. I was shouldering two apartments financially, and the bill for the loan that I took out to get out to the Southwest. At the point in which I got to Oklahoma, I wasn't sure of whether or not we would have enough money to make it back to Asheville. I tried driving to North Carolina, bed ended up stopping just outside of Nashville, Tennessee to take a break. I had stopped taking my medicine, so my symptoms were worse. I had fallen back into psychosis, and Jack and Russell were still depressed, observing their mother losing her mind. We finally got home, and I got help. Never again would I travel with my dogs. We stayed in Asheville, which became their romping ground again. Seven months after I took a billing clerk job at the Veterans Affairs in Asheville, I quit. Again, Jack and Russell were alone, even though I had a dog sitter break up the day for them while they stayed in the apartment. After all that I had gone through, I was also going through an unwanted bad experience. Everything was going wrong, and I was drinking. I moved home to my parents' house. The dogs were ecstatic. Russell perked up even though he was blind, and diabetic. Jack once again loved hikes I started a book about the mountains, and hiking, so we enjoyed nearly daily hikes through the Foothills of western North Carolina. So, when the day came when Russell went into diabetic shock, I wasn't prepared. Everything had been going well. I got Russell to the vet immediately. Three days later, he died. He was too scared to let go, so his passing was assisted. So, was Jack's passing. Jack would wander through the house, and yard looking for his brother. It took a year. Jack had cancer, and Philippe had been thrown out of a car, and landed in the trees aligning the property. I adopted him, and, then, a week later, Jack let go. He stopped eating, and appeared to be sickly, and was whining non-stop at night. I put him down. And, that was the end. Both dogs were cremated, and photos of both dogs are peppered throughout my bedroom. I still live with my parents. I still have Philippe. And, I still miss my angels, Jack and Russell. They saved me from so much, and I still cry, just as I am right now. Animals are more than pets. They're us, a reflection of the good in us, and I am encouraged by my having had Jack, and Russell in my life. I hug Philippe as much as possible. I loved them, just as I love my kitten.

# PART FIVE

# THE SCRAPBOOK

As I look at the first page of the scrapbook made in memory of my now deceased dogs, the cover gleams with a title: Jack, Russell and Me. The bottom of the cover cites: "Love is being owned by a Jack and Russell." Hearts are peppered throughout the blue book flyer, and the colors of the title bloom into what looks like a kindergartener's choice of appearance. All the same, I turn the page to the brown flyer, then to the gray first page. At the bottom of the first page reads the word, "family." And, at the top, the word, "son," appears. Two adorable little puppies are in the first picture, Jack and Russell. Jack has white fur with a black face, and Russell has brown fur. Russell is asleep, and Jack is looking doe-eyed at the camera. The two puppies are cuddled together in a small bed intended for just one small dog. A blankie also warms the dogs, and the appearance of the Bury St. Edmunds flat is that of poverty. It doesn't matter. The two puppies are loved. I turn the gray page to the white of a British decorated sheet with a picture of the two puppies, then older, resting in the back garden of the Bury St. Edmunds flat. Small attempts at gardening can be seen. Russell is laid out, relaxing in the summer sun.

Jack's ear have become prick ears, and he is attentive, albeit small. The page turns to an off white color, and the puppies are yet again inside. The living room looks sparse. But, the puppies have grown in spite of visible poverty. Russell looks directly at the camera, sitting to the side, while Jack is distracted by what looks to be a bug, tail curling. The page turns. Children's blocks spell out, "Jack," and, "Russell." The two puppies sit on my lap, both gazing at the camera with tiny bodies sitting on my legs. They have leather collars, and gorgeous, healthy coats. The page turns again to a brown paper with a picture of the two puppies showing their character. Jack's ears are tilted back, while Russell evidently growls at his brother, wiggled toward his bigger sibling. A page back to gray, the puppies show even more personality with Jack leaning to the side, ears looking vicious, and Russell looking down, as though he's dangling. The picture is the third of three. A page turns, and Jack and Russell are on the kitchen floor, both looking around for food, both attentive. In the next picture, Jack and Russell are napping on the stairs of the short stairwell of the Bury St. Edmunds flat. Russell is asleep. Jack is lying down, but with ears perked up, is awake. The next picture features Russell's nose sniffing the camera while under the bed in the master bedroom. Jack's eyes pierce the camera while he lies down next to the wall. The phrase, "fun hiding," peppers the black sheet of paper with the photograph centered. And, in the next picture, out they come. Russell's body is small, but healthy, and Jack's eyes are closed from the glare of the camera's flash. Back downstairs, the next photograph exhibits just how feisty jack russell terriers are. The toys for Jack and Russell are scattered through the rug, with the inside stuffing ripped out. Russell looks directly at the camera with love. Jack chomps on a bone, toys undone. The next picture features the same scene, but with both Jack and Russell gazing at the camera, as though they think that they have done nothing wrong. Oftentimes, I would, in the United States Air Force, have to deploy, so the next photograph shows two young children holding Jack and Russell while they were being dog sat by a friend in the military while I was on a short deployment. Russell is cuddled, leaning back, and Jack is panting, happily posing for the camera. At last, the dogs go home, still puppies. Jack and Russell, in the next picture, are in America, cuddled up on a large dog bed in my parents' house. Jack looks directly at the camera, while Russell is seemingly too sleepy to pose for the picture. The next picture features Russell chewing on his beloved bone, while yet another picture has Russell sniffing the camera while showing the bone, bed, and blankie with his brown eyes gleaming at the light of the flash. The next picture is of Jack looking down, tired, next to his bed. And, the next page of the scrapbook features both dogs once again snuggling together, grooming each other in front of the wood burning fireplace in the Zebulon, North Carolina living room. The page turns, and, for the first time, the mini-pin is shown playing with Jack and Russell. Jack watches her with attentive ears, while Russell simply chews on a bone. The bone chewing ends, and it was time for fun. Russell is shown pulling on a toy with the mini-pin, and Jack has the bone. The next photograph features the boxer lying down on Jack and Russell's two smaller beds, while Jack, and Russell sleep, cuddled up, on the boxer's large, brown bed, still in the living room. As time went by, I went home, and was home for Christmas. At the end of the scrapbook, and Jack and Russell's first year of life, Christmas decoration align the fireplace, and Jack, and Russell are on the loveseat, snuggled up together, with Jack's eyes bled out, and with Russell chewing on a bone. The next Christmas photograph shows Jack in a Santa hat, looking tortured, while sitting on one of the kitchen chairs for the pose. And, of course, there is the hysterical photograph of Russell looking like he had had too much egg nog. His hat nearly coming off, Russell is standing up, as though he wants to get down, off of the chair. The Christmas morning picture come next, with Jack's body stretched out, with him sniffing a Christmas morning toy. The mini-pin is seated in my lap in the following photograph, with Jack distracted by the plethora of toys scattered over the wood floor. Russell stretches his body out, trying to take a toy from the loveseat in the next picture. Jack gets ahold of his stuffed animals in the next photograph, and then both Jack, and Russell wear their stockings around their necks in the next two photographs. Toys, and Christmas had, it was time to sit on grandpa's lap. Russell relaxes, while Jack tried to lick, and kiss grandpa's face. Then, both dogs get onto grandpa's lap, and kiss each other. The final photograph is of the summer, with Jack prancing around the back deck . . .

# PART SIX

# PHILIPPE

THE SUMMERS IN WESTERN NORTH CAROLINA HAD grown increasingly hot. In July, Jack was mainly in the house, cool, and wearing pampers due to his numerous illnesses, and subsequent problems keeping his bladder controlled. I was on the computer, typing up a book that was going to be released, at the time, very soon, and my parents were outside.

"Rebecca, can you come help up with the cat," my father said.

I immediately responded to the call for help, and saw that my parents had taken a dog crate out from the basement to help keep a kitten safe. The kitten had been thrown out of a passing car, into the trees, and was meowing. My mother heard the kitten, then my father got the kitten out of the trees.

"Go get her some dog food, and milk," my father demanded.

I made a dish for the kitten. My parents got themselves together that morning, and then took the kitten to the animal shelter. No kittens were being taken, so then I went to a local animal rescue facility with the kitten. The rescue only accepted dogs.

"You can take kittens to Brother Wolf," the rescue facilitator said.

I felt bad for the kitten, so I took her home. I went to Walmart to purchase girl-inspired items for cats, and went back home. With all of the necessities, I went to the vet.

"It looks like you have a little boy," the vet said.

"Oh, okay, I guess that I can replace his items."

I had purchased pink everything, so I held the kitten, thought about adopting the little boy, and did.

"I'd like to name him Philippe," I said.

French for 'love of horses,' I had adopted a black kitten. We went to the pet store together, and I purchased everything in sight. It took a month before the kitten would eat the luxury food that I had purchased. I didn't know anything about cats, so I read a lot. Jack died a week into me having Philippe. And, Philippe was sad. He liked playing with Jack; that I could tell. But, with Philippe in the world, I had to comfort a whimpering kitten, raise him, so that he would have a chance at a happy, healthy life.

---

I considered not writing about Philippe. But, he's dead. I made the mistake of putting stickers all over my car citing that I loved my cat. He was a year old, and was killed. He's buried in the backyard. I'm pet-less. Writing about Philippe seems to be something that I need to do. He was my first cat. I will adopt others, but not for some time. I took Philippe hiking, walking, shopping, any, and everything that he could do. He ate luxury food. He was spoiled with countless toys. I had planned to carry him during a holiday parade, but he's dead. He's dead. And, I want to keep his memories safe, unknown to people who apparently hate cats, even perfect ones. He was my only cat, my only love for a kitten. He's dead . . .

# THE END

"Rebecca, can you come out here, and help with the cat?" "The cat?" "Just come out here, and help." "Okay, one second." "Oh, my goodness, it's a little kitten." "Yes." "We're going to take him to the animal shelter on the way." "Okay." "What happened?" "The animal shelter has a sign on the front door: NO KITTENS." "Oh, I can try the rescue right down the road." "Thank you. That would help." "Do you take cats?" "No, we're a dog rescue. Cats wouldn't fair well here, as you can hear." "Okay, thank you." "My parents found this kitten on our property, and I think that he needs help. Is there a rescue that can take him?" "Yes, but they're closed today." "I don't know if he's a girl, or a boy. I went crazy in Walmart. I think that she's a girl." "No, it looks like you have a little boy cat. I could be wrong, but . . ." "Oh, then I guess that I need to change the crate. It's pink." "Yeah." "Jack has late stage cancer. There's a drug that can help these little guys ease . . ." "Hello?" "This little guy's been through everything medically." "Well, it's you, and me." "Meow." We spent months in the study, away from the poodle who seemed agitated by little Philippe. Eventually, Philippe came out of the room where he had been for three months, large enough to not be eaten by a hunting dog. We had been going on trips to a pet retail store for fun. Philippe would stay in the black tote, popping his little head out of the bag to see the wonders of treats, food, and toys for cats. Being a kitten, Philippe didn't know that hiking as a cat at Lake James was different. "I have four cats." "Yeah." "It's unusual to see them out on a trail." At a young age, Philippe saw a lake, and even hiked all the way to Tom's Creek's waterfall. He didn't seem to mind. "Oh, look, he looks just like ours." I had decided to take Philippe downtown during the Christmas parade, and had to ready his nerves, so we walked up and down the streets of Marion. "Lady, that's animal cruelty." "It's not animal cruelty. She has to get that cat ready for the parade." Over time, Philippe's hormones caused instability in his behavior. "Is this normal?" "No." He received medicine for anger, and had special air dispensers for his mood. "You've got an angry kitty?" "Yes." All the same, we continued to journey into the surrounding area. "Meow." "Okay, sweet pea." Philippe stretched out his forearms at Lake Tomahawk in Black Mountain, just as a child would; I picked him up. We would go anywhere, and everywhere together. I took him to a hardware store looking for plants. "My cat would go crazy if I did that." I loved my kitten. Philippe eventually enjoyed the car rides, climbing throughout my SUV. He loved to look around, and see where we were headed next. The poodle calmed down. Philippe started to flip and flop on the floor, rolling onto his back, and side. He even played with the poodle. "Mom, don't let Philippe outside." "Oh, crap. I'm sorry." "Dad." "Philippe. Philippe. Come here. Come on." "Rebecca, he's crying at the door. You need to go on, and just let him out." "Okay." "Philippe, why don't you go in your litter box? Silly bee. You're trying to keep up with the dogs." "Meow." "Okay, Philippe. Come on in. It's late." "I can hear Philippe around midnight, outside." "Yeah, he's staying out later, and later." "Come on, sweetie, let's go to bed in my bed." "Meow." "He purrs on my bad, and presses his paws into my body. It's cute." "He's staying out all night long." "I know. I don't know what's going on with him." "Rebecca, Philippe's dead." "What?" "Philippe's dead." "Jesus Christ. Why is this happening? Why?" "Your father is going to bury him in the backyard." "I don't want to see him." "He's buried." I looked around my room at the images of black cats, each photograph reminding me of Philippe. I cried for months. Presently, I have no dog, and no cat. My children are dead, and replacing them seems like something that I just cannot do. I'm a surrogate to the poodle now, but dream about Jack and Russell, and hate sleeping without my kitten. They're all gone. It's time to grow. I'm becoming a parent to human children who will learn about how special it is to have an animal look to you for essential needs, yes, but love, also. They'll learn about how to care for animals, how to love them, and how to never let go.

# THE AFTERLIFE

I NO LONGER DRINK ALCOHOL, NOR DO I DATE. I BLAME myself in part for losing Jack and Russell in such a way that was painful for them, and for not being able to keep Philippe safe. I'm moving on. Slowly. To rectify wrongs, I now work with local non-profits geared toward the rescue and care of homeless or abused pets. I drive all over the country relocating those animals, giving them a chance at a forever home. Oddly, I don't feel the sorrow that I felt a year ago, even with so much of the media focusing on loss due to COVID-19. My awful scenario has resolved, and I'm looking at adopting real children, not just furry ones. I'm destined to teach my children the in's and out's of fostering fur babies. Yes, fostering. I can't fathom adopting another pair of puppies, or having a house filled with kittens with the notion that they would replace Jack, Russell, and Philippe. So, as a family, we'll care for the needs of animals who need a nice experience rather than a shelter life. I suppose that I wrote this book more so for them, and not for myself. I've already resolved to keep up with volunteering for the non-profits I work with, even though I'm going into nursing, then law, and then, again, into medicine. I'm hesitant to leave this new life of kissing homeless puppies, and snuggling with kittens up. I think that whoever my children will be, they will appreciate the work of the non-profit world. I'm more so thinking of them now, instead of loss. My future children give me a sense of hope. And, they will be my next chapter. I've resolved to be cautious with dating, waiting until the man respects my faith, that of Catholicism. So far, no dating has happened, but I still think that fairy tales can happen, even at forty years of age. But, of course, I'm focused wholly on my children who are in a home needing a foster mother. That's the end, I suppose. I can't thank my darling pets enough. They taught me how to be patient, responsible, and happy. It's time to move on. It's time to live again. I'm coming out of the grief mixed with depression. My next adventure is nursing school, as well as children. I can't thank my fur babies enough. And, I don't think that their lives should be taken lightly. However, I'm moving on, with love in heart and mind.

# LILY

Being a fan of Edith Wharton's *The House of Mirth*, I reveled in the main character's name, Lily, as in Lily Bart. Seeing the pins filled with puppies in front of the Ingles in Sylva, North Carolina tempted me to adopt yet another dog, not just Jack and Russell. I called the main line for the adoption center, a home where dozens of abandoned animals were cared for. The house smelled like a barn yard, but the couple running the rescue could not have been more kind.

"I think that I'll take this one."

"Just one. Go ahead and grab two."

"No, I already have two dogs."

In the vet's office, I named Lily for the literary character. Lily was strong, and lucky. She would kiss me with sweet little licks on the cusp of my neck, looking for milk presumably. I was elated to bring her home to my two-bedroom, upper level apartment where Jack and Russell lived.

"Jack, Russell, stop it."

I cradled Lily high in the air, aware from my embarrassingly jealous dogs who jumped to snip at my new puppy. In time, Jack and Russell grew to accept Lily, especially after I moved from the riverside apartment to a house in the deeper woodland area of Cullohwee. There was a sliding door that I could leave open, and I fenced in the yard stemming off of the deck. Lily, Jack, and Russell were safe. And, for two years, our life was perfect. We all went on hikes. We went for rides. The dogs would stay in luxury accommodations while I travelled to Europe and Mexico. In Zebulon, Lily would play with the boxer Bedford, and leave the miniature pin, Mini, alone. But, Jack was depressed. He went from being carried around, to struggling for attention. I realized that I had made a mistake, that my two dogs were enough for one person. I asked family if they would take in Lily; they did not. Desperate, I tried to make it work. Of course, when you're young, and unaware of how stressful three children can be, mistakes are to be made. I took Lily to the shelter in Haywood County where I knew she would not be killed due to their low population, and active animal rescue.

"Come on, Lily. It's okay."

Lily's hound nature made her hard to handle, so I gave the clerk a book that I had purchased entitled, *How to Control Your Uncontrollable Dog.* Lily was trained in every way, but three dogs were still too much. It was time to let go, and give Jack back his place in the alpha chain.

"Come on, sweetie."

"We'll keep her here, but, you know, we can't keep her forever."

"I know. She's a good dog. She'll find a good home."

Later that evening, I went to Walmart. There was a little girl who was buying a collar and leash for her new, female dog. I was relieved after realizing that her father had allowed her to adopt Lily. I didn't say anything. But, deep in my heart, I wanted to cry. I had made a huge mistake that my father first recognized. Bedford lost his playmate, and everything seemed to capsize after Lily was away with her new family. Jack and Russell adapted well to the change, but I didn't. I drank consistently for a month before giving up on wine completely. It wasn't Lily's fault. I should have known better than to adopt another dog. Some part of me misses her still today. She was a good dog, who deserved a good, permanent home that I couldn't give her.

Years later, I tried adopting a third dog with Jack and Russell still in my life. My father said 'no' in a very elaborate way (i.e. slamming doors). The dog was returned to the shelter the next day. I paid for the dog's adoption fees so that she would be available with no purchase required. Today, I have no pets. No cats; no dogs. I work with the American Humane Society weekly, which, I've found, is the best way for me, being mentally ill, to experience the joy of animal care. However, I do have two dogs who I can care for who are not attached to anything that I do up in Asheville, North Carolina. Their names are C. C. and Winston, and I am their surrogate now, living in Nebo, North Carolina, out in the countryside where they enjoy a good bark and a good hunt. They have become my children. I ensure that they are fed premium foods, and get exercise. C. C. is a poodle, and Winston is a red doberman. Their stories will follow.

# WINSTON, AND THEN, C. C.

LARGE, WINSTON HAD ALREADY GROWN INTO HIS ADULT weight before moving to Marion from Zebulon, North Carolina. His tail clipped, it was a nub, but Winston's ears were left undone. A Red Doberman, Winston was roughly 100 pounds of pure muscle with short fur and a brown-reddish hue to his coat.

"I think that we'll call him 'Winston' after Winston Churchill. He was a red head," my father said.

My mother had to move to the Marion house in North Carolina because, due to the Great Recession, she has lost her job at Dorthea Dix Hospital, which shut down and moved to Butner just outside of Chapel Hill. The problem was that she lived in Zebulon with my father, a two hour commute to Butner would follow with her accepting a job at the brand new hospital. Cherry Hospital, the other mental institution, was also two hours away. Ultimately, my mother chose to move away from my father in Zebulon, and live in the retirement home in Marion, work at Broughton Hospital in Morganton, and stay there for two years, separated from my father who still had to finish out work at a pharmaceutical company in Clayton, in the Piedmont. My mother and father decided to send the grown puppy to Marion, in the Foothills of Western North Carolina, where he could run on nearly five acres of land, and not be bound to a house and small yard. Jack and Russell didn't seem to mind Winston, accepting him into their clan, and eating his food, which was rich compared to their diet kibble.

---

The television news blared into the living area while Winston misbehaved by harassing Jack and Russell, so, as one does, I locked Winston in his cage for a time out. What sounded like whining, stating the sound of, "You're not my mother," began. Winston was very vocal in his protest to punitive actions against his snarling over Jack and Russell. Eventually, Winston calmed down, and I released the iron cage lock to let Winston back out into the house. He was very much so not pleased.

The property we lived on had roughly five acres with everything from a flower field to a vegetable garden to a series of foreign gardens to, as it were, chickens. Every day, I had to tend the chickens. And, every day, Winston would bite my feet, being a puppy still, along the way to and back from the chicken coup.

"Stop!"

Winston would just bark.

"Stop! I said, 'Stop!'"

My father's absence made Winston wild. When my father retired, and finally moved to his retirement home, Winston stopped biting feet.

---

It was summer, and I wanted to go for a walk with Jack and Russell around the property's field (six times around amounted to a mile). Elated, Jack and Russell were bouncing around, wiggling and wagging. Winston expressed his elation by going outside and running down and back from the end of the field. On one trip, Winston umped on my back, trying to push me forward. I fell to the ground, on hands and knees, and got hurt. A driver by the property slowed, but passed by when he or she realized that I was okay. I couldn't believe Winston, and was surprised by his strength.

---

Winston expelled a lot of energy when he was young. Oftentimes, he would trample flowers, dig, and insatiably bark at anyone coming into the driveway in Marion.

"#%@!" my mother would yell. "If you don't stop digging in the garden, I'm taking you to the pound."

Winston would jump, run around, and then proceed to step on newly planted flowers with his large paws. I wondered if my mother was serious. I would simply keep my Jack and Russell out of the excitement, and away from the gardens.

---

Jack and Russell had aged, so keeping them on a leash was no longer necessary, nor disciplining them. Winston was still wild, however. My father's solution? A shock collar for behavior and fencing.

The invisible fence was installed. Winston obeyed its boundaries. He also knew to behave when he saw his obedience collar.

"Now you'll calm down," my father would say. "I'm going to shock you."

Feet-biting stopped. Winston wore the training collar, and I noticed that his mood would change.

"Dad, I don't think that Winston likes his shock collar."

"I know. He gets depressed. Here," my father would take the collar off once the assurance of good behavior was had.

---

"Stop, Winston," I yelled.

Winston got into bopping Jack and Russell with his nose. Russell and Jack would growl. I would take two fingers and spank his rear end.

"Stop it! Bad Winston!"

Winston never stopped the behavior, even when Jack and Russell had developed ailments. Russell was blind, at one point, and Jack was nearly blind. All the same, it was Winston's favorite way of greeting the much smaller dogs, a behavior that I was never able to correct.

---

Every day except Sunday, something happens. And, at the time, and still today, Winston knows it. What am I talking about? The mail is delivered. And, anyone with a dog knows that the delivery of the mail causes quite a stir. For Winston, the delivery of the mail entails barking, running, challenging the invisible fence, and all of the rest. Now, if mail is delivered by UPS or Fedex, Winston knows. For one, he's on attack mode. And, once the box is delivered, he had to bite the box, and try to rip it into shreds, carrying it into the air, and slinging it to the ground. In Marion, Winston would run the length of the field to chase the postal worker or delivery person. Why? I don't know. I don't think that anyone know who has a high strung dog for a pet.

---

Every dog has a spot. Winston, after experimenting one the floor of the study, found his in the field near the vegetable garden. It took about two years to train him to use the outdoor restroom instead of the indoors. Strangely, Philippe refused to use his litter box, but, instead, used the dirt in the flower garden in the front. Why? Again, I don't know.

---

My father's affection for squirrels excited both C. C. and Winston. While Jack and Russell remained disinterested in the furry creatures of the back garden's bird feeder, (even though Jack successfully caught, killed, and ate one of the rodents).

"Squirrel. Squirrel. Go get it. Squirrel," my father would say.

C. C. and Winston would proceed to bark and run out of the front door, run around to the back yard, and, of course, sniff the ground around the bird feeder after all was said and done and the squirrels had found a treetop hiding place. This was nearly a daily occurrence that Jack and Russell ignored. Philippe? He killed birds.

---

There is no greater pleasure than a wet nose and a licking kiss from a dog who one might feel as though he or she does not love him or her. Winston, after Jack, Russell, and Philippe had passed, began giving me we nose kisses while I was still in bed, in the morning.

"Give me a kiss," I would say in the living room while scratching Winston, who had developed allergies and itchy skin. Winston would oblige. I would laugh.

---

When people pass away, there's a sense of disbelief. With Winston, it was the same when Jack and Russell and Philippe passed away. Russell died first. Winston, having loved Russell (even with the agitating nose bopping) kept looking for him in the house and around the property. The same thing happened when Jack was put to sleep. Winston did not handle their passing well. They both were cremated, so Winston had no way of knowing if Jack and Russell were alive or not. He became depressed. He whined and took his paw up to signal that he missed them both each time. Probably because I was so distraught, crying and heaving. When Philippe died, Winston ran to the box that his corpse was in and wanted to play. All the same, that day,

Winston whined, took his paw up to take my hand, and then gave me a hug by leaning his neck and head into my arms.

---

C. C. was initially named Clementine, a formal name that she kept. When she was a puppy, and introduced to Winston, he adored her. They were instant playmates, enjoying the five acres together.

"Can you believe that Winston is such a good brother?" my mother would ask. "Look at him."

Winston would smell C. C.'s ears when they were infected, let her eat out of his bowl, and gallop around the field with her. There could not have been a more loving brother.

---

A tall, limber dog, Winston would run the field, oftentimes to his detriment. Both his right and left legs were torn, and, so, my father took him to the vet.

"He's a bionic dog," my father said the next day after Winston had had his surgery.

"Winston, you're weird," I would say.

"He's being silly," my mother would say.

Winston's nub would wagged. He was the center of attention.

---

Wearing a nursing uniform, my mother said, "Okay, Winston, it's time to go to work.

Jack and Russell wagged their tails and smiled. Two o'clock every day my mother would drink her last cup of coffee and head down the road to Broughton Hospital in Morganton, North Carolina. Her shift would las until the midnight hour, so, on this evening, I decided to take Winston, Jack, and Russell for a ride in my brand new 2018 Ford Escape. Winston jumped into the small SUV's backseat, filling up the entire seat. Russell sat on the floor of the backseat, and Jack took shotgun. Winston was silent. This was his first ride since moving to Marion.

"Winston, what's wrong?"

Whining, and with me being alarmed, I stopped at Marion's new Walmart, and opened the back door.

"Oh, God. Winston, get back here. Now. There you go. Now get in," I said.

Easier said than done, I suddenly feared that Winston was going to take off.

"No, God, no."

Finally, Winston was in the car again. We drove 30 minutes away to the psychiatric institution.

"Mom, I'm outside, and I have a surprise."

"Okay, let me get my round done. I'll be out in a minute."

The call ended.

"Winston, isn't this exciting. We get to see mom."

The door to the smaller building opened. My mother walked out.

"Oh, hey, Winston. You got to go for a ride."

"He did."

I didn't tell my mother about the fiasco of almost losing Winston in the Walmart parking lot.

"I can take him here every night if you want me to."

"That'd be fine."

So, Winston started to go for rides.

"Winston, stop it," my father said. "See, that's why I can't stand taking you anywhere."

Winston's nub wagged.

"Okay, it's time to go to the vet."

The vet's office was the only place that Winston would go after his bionic surgery, which limited him to five acres and produced a lot of anxiety.

---

A car honked. Winston barked.

"Winston," I yelled.

Winston ran to the door.

"Winston, get back. Back."

His sheer strength nudged me out of the way. Someone waved from the car, wanting to buy eggs. Winston challenged the electric fence.

"Sorry, he gets excited. What can I do for you?"

"I just need one dozen eggs."

"Okay, I'll be right back. Winston, stop!"

As I went down to the second level of the house, Winston continued guarding the property through aggression in the form of intimidating barking.

"Okay, here you go. Sorry about the dog. That'll be two dollars."

"That's okay. Here you go."

The car left. Winston ran to the edge of the Marion house and continued barking.

"Winston! Winston, get inside!"

Ignoring my request, Winston darted off to the end of the field, chasing the car alongside of Nix Creek Road. I went inside. Minutes later, Winston returned, jumped on the latch of the front door, and let himself in.

------

While snapping green beans, someone knocked on the door. I immediately went to corral Winston into his cage, locking the latch. My father stepped outside. Winston roared with a loud whine, grabbing the door of his cage with his paw. Once my father came back in, I unlocked Winston's cage. He ran spritely toward the door, jumping, and then barging outside onto the deck, running toward the driveway. Content, Winston, in time, came back in.

------

On a cool summer day, Winston, C. C., Jack, and Russell were outside, assisting with the care of the chickens. I heard a loud honk, and looked up. My father was already walking toward the vehicle as Winston ran toward the front yard. I could only hear barking, violent barking. As I walked to the front, I saw Winston snapping at a man on a scooter. The visitor was in the yard, passed the line for the electric fence, wearing a helmet, and trying to follow my father's instruction of backing up to the end of the driveway. Winston went wild. As the scooter reversed, Winston ran around the scooter, barking and nearly biting the guest. Eventually, the man was behind the line, and in safety.

"I thought that Winston was going to kill him," my father later told my mother.

"Winston, were you going to kill him?" my mother asked.

"Arlene, it isn't funny."

"Yeah, Winston went nuts," I said.

———————

Oftentimes, Nix Creek Road required service from the McDowell Department of Transportation. One day, loud trucks with beeping sounds woke up Winston, and he went to the edge of the front yard, to the road to investigate. Barking, the DOT workers laughed.

"If you keep barking and being cute, I'm going to throw you into the back of the truck, and take you home."

"Winston! Winston, get in the house," I demanded.

Winston came running onto the porch, nearly knocking over a blind Russell who then growled.

———————

My grandfather had welts. I have welts, lumps of fat. Winston, over time, joined the family tradition. Bumpy, he would go through routine check-ups, making sure that his welts weren't cancer. Jack had welts. It was cancer. Someday, I am anticipating that Winston's welts, the samples, will come back positive. Not only does he have welts, his spine is collapsing, so he pants when he's in pain from laying down the wrong way. He takes medication for pain, not just for the allergies. Someday, I'll wake up, and Winston won't greet me, a reality that I'm prepared for, for now.

---

As grooming goes, Winston is bathed in a walk-in shower. I have not tried to clip his nails since he growled and nearly nipped me over my touching his claws on one paw. My mother bathed him while showing in Marion. Here, in Nebo, he's yet to see a bath. Winston has to be sedated for anyone to touch his nails, so he, of course, goes to the vet's office for nail care.

---

The early days would come to mind, namely in remembering how much Winston loved his rides to see my mother. Unfortunately, after he tore his legs, and became bionic, he could no longer jump into the car. My father would have to lift him. Alas, Winston developed anxiety, even on the five acre farm. In Nebo, he is no different, just as anxious as he was in Marion.

---

In Marion, the farm was large enough to run around and roam. In Nebo, there is a lot less land that is clear. Most of the property is wooded. Still, Winston wanders through the woods, expelling that anxiety. Once in a while, cars drive up or down the roadway leading to the driveway. The sound of an engine excites Winston into a panic, and he takes up the old job of barking at cars coming and going. Restricted by yet another electric fence, Winston is retrained from going to the road. His other stress relieving activities entail going out of the garage door at night so that he can hunt raccoons. Sniffing the ground, he never catches one, but enjoys the chase, seemingly. My father catches his nighttime ritual with a night vision camera. Winston seems to do a lot more raccoon hunting in Nebo. Winston was also switched to a new, more expensive food. With the old food, Winston would rarely eat. He seemed to enjoy the change that I funded. On a sensitive skin and stomach diet, he also cannot eat lamb. So, he eats chicken-based kibble. Event with the special diet meals, Winston still gets a pill, shot, and other allergy medicine. My father routinely goes to the vet's office to purchase the rather expensive items. And, with the meds, Winston has nightly difficulties. Around 11 or one in the morning, Winston goes out of the house to keep up an old habit: nighttime piddles. My father is the primary caretaker in that regard, getting up, and sitting up until Winston returns from his sniffing and tinkling. Yet another steady habit is his knee-sitting. If Winston likes you, he will sit on one knee, and, in time, fall asleep while rested. He loves kisses and scratching, and lets you know by a big lick to the face. His loving demeanor is oftentimes rewarded with bits of lunch meat. Taking anything out of the refrigerator causes him to follow right behind you, letting you know that he's hungry, too. Winston can also be rude, however. Not fighting with C. C., he would get into spats with Philippe, leaving Winston's nose bloodied after being scratched by my cat. But, of course, I am sure that you know about the historic fight between cats and dogs. Winston seemed to miss Philippe, even though they did fight. Each time you lose a pet, animals grieve, too, just in a less pronounced way.

Winston was welcomed by Jack and Russell when he was a puppy. Winston welcomed C. C. when she arrived. Both Winston and C. C. were skeptical of Philippe. Jack just growled at Philippe's hissing. C. C.? Well, to memory, she was the terrier, wanting to hunt Philippe as a kitten rather than welcome him. To C. C.'s credit, Jack and Russell greeted her with growls and biting when she was a puppy, so she learned to loathe newcomers. C. C. also took up Winston's old trick by jumping, and trying to knock me down. At one point, C. C. jumped through the air, poodle fur flowing, and knocked Russell completely out of my arms. Blind, Russell was completely confused. I tried to discipline C. C., but she simply kept running in a large circle, smiling, and barking. I took Russell inside, and ignored the bad behavior.

C. C.'s wild youth also led her to periodically chase the chickens on the farm in Marion. Whenever one, or more, of the chickens escaped the coup, C. C. would gallop toward them, attempting to grab them with her mouth, but then change course and merely bully them with barking. My father was never pleased. In Nebo, there are baby chicks. And, of course, C. C. hunts them, listening to the peeping coming from the new coup built (and poodle and raccoon proofed) by my father and his woodworking and construction abilities.

To expel C. C.'s energy, my mother would take C. C., her dog, for walks at the YMCA routinely. C. C. loved to go for walks. She started with a color, and a lot of wild behavior, but later was put in a more comfortable harness that kept her away from other dogs, which she did not seem to care for.

Hikes eventually came, which settled her down. My mother and father went on five mild hikes with C. C., something that she seemed to bean over before and after the hikes. Her puppy days were not always so pleasant, however. One evening, C. C. was sitting on my lap in a recliner in the house in Marion. When the chair went down, she caught her leg in the front of the chair and began to wail and cry. She limped for a bit, and no hospital visit was necessary, fortunately. Also in Marion, C. C. simply could not stand Philippe. Philippe, once old enough to not be eaten alive, would run from one end of the house to the other—under beds, behind the couch, and into the study where C. C. could not chase him. Ultimately, C. C., being a poodle, wanted to kill him, or, so I thought. On one occasion, I pulled Philippe, then only three month old, out from under the bed in my parents' bedroom, on my stomach, on the floor. I thought that C. C. was going to snap at him. Instead? What did she do? Licked him. Apparently, C. C. wanted a kitten to rear, but Philippe did not want her to be his mother, oftentimes hitting her nose with his paw repeatedly, and then running away.

C. C. took Philippe's death hard, as was the case with Jack and Russell's passing. To soothe her, I would take her from the Marion property to local trails to go for hikes when my parents started to spend more time volunteering to do trail work in the local area. Fat, I could not hike for very long, but C. C.'s mood lifted, all the same. Now, in Nebo, C. C. goes for daily walks up and down the nearby paved hill, with mountain views and plenty of rabbits to hunt and chase . . .

. . . my stomach growls while I am seated in a small recliner while listening to music. I close the recliner, get up, and go get the chair for the writing desk, from the sewing room, where it was moved for a sewing project. I am writing. It's Friday, Lent, and I am fasting. C. C.? She's sprawled out on her bed in the study in the Nebo house. Palm Sunday is ahead of us . . .

"If you could go back in time, would you, having spent nearly 30 years as a nurse, work with people or animals?"

"I don't know. Animals are easier to deal with, I think. People are complicated. An animal just needs food, shelter, and warmth. That's it. With people, you never know what you're going to get. They bottle things, like anger. You just really never know what's going on with them until they lash out."

"Cats do that."

"Well, their ears go back, you know."

"I just think that working with people might not be such a good thing for me. With the paranoid schizophrenia, I hear things on top of what people are saying."

"And that doesn't happen with animals?"

"No, I'm completely calm with animals. I just think that being an occupational therapy assistant or nurse just isn't in my future anymore. They have a vet tech program in Asheville that I'm interested in. With animals, I'd go all of the way, be a doctor, a vet."

"Yeah, I thought that I was going to be a doctor, but then reality hit—all of the time and work, study just wasn't worth it."

"I like animals. I'm always happy when I go to work with them."

The latch to the leash clicked. C. C. immediately pulled, trying to force me down the driveway at a faster pace.

"Okay, C. C., time to go for a walk."

C. C.'s ears and poodle fur blew back as she and I meandered down the long gravel and dirt driveway toward the road just off of the edge of the property. Once at the road, C. C. stopped.

"What is it, C. C.? Are you hunting rabbits again? Do you have the scent?"

C. C. periodically stopped, sniffed the ground, even licking leaves of grass. I no longer missed Jack, Russell, and Philippe. C. C. had become my furry friend. Since I no longer drink alcohol, and now eat meat, C. C. lives with me in the study during the day, when I am writing. We go for walks, hikes, and rides. My father still takes her to the groomer. I still look at a pictures of Jack and Russell that is on the wall of the study, and feel content. I cared for them well. They did actually have a good life. And, so did Philippe. C. C. is my next adventure with rearing an animal, and that's a new beginning and end for me.

"C. C., what are you doing?"

C. C. whined as we walked passed a howling hound at the end of the road, at the neighbor's house, and at the bottom of the long hill. Walking back up always is difficult. C. C. literally pulls while I lag behind, taking breaks as I inch forward. Eventually, I am back in the yard, and, out of breath, I soothe C. C.

"Okay, C. C. That's it."

I feed C. C. and Winston, give them their treats, and, later on the evening, I share my dessert (usually meat and cheese) with C. C. She falls asleep in the study, but wanders back to my parents' bedroom around midnight when Winston gets up to go outside. We are, indeed, a happy family. And, my friends, I hope that you, too, are keen at taking care of your animals.

# AND, THEN THERE WAS MISS SCARLETT

"Hi, this is Rebecca Pace. We're here waiting on the giant schnauzer puppies, and I was wondering if I'm in the right place. The Petsmart parking lot, right?"

"Yeah, we're over on the divide, in the grass with a big pin filled with puppies."

"Oh, okay. I just wanted to make sure that I'm in the right place."

We, my mother and I, had driven out to Knoxville, Tennessee after I paid over two thousand dollars for a giant schnauzer puppy who I would name Scarlett after Scarlett in *Gone With the Wind*. The puppies were calm for the most part, but Scarlett was feisty.

"I've got the runt in here, if you would prefer her."

"No, I like the feisty one."

"Okay, here you go."

Scarlett and I immediately bonded, with me kissing her, and her kissing me back with three licks. I held her like she was an infant, rocking her, bouncing a little, and then kissing her again. We left to go back home and the breeder forgot that I had already paid the full amount, knowing that I wanted Scarlett before she was available for rearing in a new home.

"You didn't pay for your dog."

"The $2,120?"

"Yes."

"We paid in full over a month ago."

"Oh, that's right. Sorry. I got sidetracked and forgot. I just wanted to say, 'Goodbye.'"

"Okay, well, everything's fine. Scarlett's napping."

That would be the last time that the breeder would see Scarlett. For the first week, all I recall is taking Scarlett outside to use the potty about every thirty minutes. Initially, Winston and C.C. acted out, not accepting Scarlett.

"Stop that," my father disciplined Winston.

"C.C. and Scarlett were playing hard, so she should get a good night's sleep," my father said.

"Can I hold her?" my friend's child asked.

"Look, Scarlett, look at the mountain," I said.

"Scarlett did good on the hike today," my mother said.

The day I got Scarlett, I resolved to stop drinking, to survive that bad time. For the most part, I've kept that promise to Scarlett. For three days, I failed, and Scarlett let me know. But, now, we go on daily walks, she has a good routine, and she's even housetrained. Things are easier now. Scarlett's stopped teething, and she is doing well with her training, the puppy kindergarten that I take her to on Saturday afternoons. She knows the command, sit. And, we play tug-of-war daily. She's chewing on treats instead of the furniture, and she's excellent with children, something that I was concerned about.

"Play, Scarlett. Go swimming."

Scarlett, black and hot from the sunshine at Lake James, just stood there, panting, even though the water was within a foot of her feet. She seemed scared of the waves from the boats zooming by, but fascinated by the families splashing in the brown water with a glistening reflection. I was in hiking gear. And, we had just hiked one mile around a flat trail. Scarlett stopped every five minutes or so, sniffing and wanting to play with the fauna.

"Look, Scarlett, there's a turtle."

"Okay, sweetie, here's your treat, and water."

"Cradle your puppy," the training instructor said.

"Scarlett, come here."

I picked Scarlett up, holding her on my lap.

"Okay, when I say, 'Cradle your puppy,' that means that you hold your puppy, and massage its ears, paws, or shoulders. You should start to notice that your puppy will fall asleep."

"Sit. Yes."

I handed a piece of cheese to Scarlett as she kept sitting on command.

I'm not going to lie. Raising a giant schnauzer puppy has been difficult, like raising Jack and Russell. But, I love Scarlett. I don't hit her. I use commands. Sometimes she rebels, but that's usually due to a lack of exercise, so she walks at least a mile a day. I had high hopes two days ago that she would walk more than a mile, but the heat depresses her, and we end up back at the car. Someday, we'll hike five mile trails. Just not now. I love my puppy, and I can't imagine life without her now. So much so, that I'm registering her as an emotional support animal.

I'm living again. Scarlett has brought joy back into my life. And, that is the end of this beginning. Maybe, dear reader, you can find elation, too, with the adoption of a dog or cat.

# FINALE

It's Saturday, the 17ᵀᴴ of July, nearly three years since Jack passed, and four since Russell was put to sleep. Scarlett is growing. She's four months now, and healthy, thankfully. Scarlett is now the light of my life. I'm due to foster-to-adopt two little girls to start my adventure in being a human child mother. Eventually, I'd like to adopt as many as the state of North Carolina will allow. Of course, I'll teach my children to respect and love animals. We're adopting cats from the animal shelter, and I've put in an inquiry to adopt an airedale terrier. I thought that I'd finish this memoir with a sweeping scene of my hiking with Scarlett out to Art Loeb on the Blue Ridge Parkway, sprinkling Jack and Russell's ashes, and leaving a photo of Philippe (he was buried), but, simply put, I couldn't stand the thought of losing them again, leaving behind what I have left of those memories. Scarlett seems to understand that I had other pets. She looks at me as though she wants me to give her the attention I gave Jack, Russell, and Philippe. I've made a committed to stop grieving, to stop letting the regrets of the past haunt me, for her. We walk every day. She's well fed, and adored, but there is just something that still hurts. I still cry about Jack and Russell, even Philippe. The pain is depressing. And, Scarlett bites me to let me know that I need to live. I know that I do, and, of course, I will strive to live for her now, for my future children, for the other puppy and kittens, for myself.

The alarm on my phone rang at six o'clock. Scarlett hardly moved. I hit the snooze feature and went back to bed for fifteen minutes. The alarm rang again. Scarlett's docked tail wagged as I moved to sit up.

"Okay, Scarlett, time to get up."

Scarlett jumped off of the bed. The shrine to Jack, Russell, and Philippe just feet away remained undisturbed. After letting Scarlett out for a potty break at five, I was still tired at six. All the same, I fed Scarlett, let her bite C. C.'s legs, and Winston wandered around the kitchen looking for his meal. The day begins this way every day. Scarlett chows down on her soft and dry food, sniffs outside, plays with C. C., and my parents yell at Scarlett for stirring up the morning. I rest in the study, watching the morning news, and Scarlett visits occasionally, focused more so on her morning chew stick and chicken jerky treat that she has in the living room. Today, Scarlett and I will walk, I'll write, she'll continue to bite C. C.'s legs and Winston's ears. If it's a particularly good day, we'll even go for a hike. That's only if I have nothing to do with my writing assignments, language learning, or studying for nursing school and the LSAT. I left my job at the rescue. Scarlett didn't like my absence, so I'm wholly committed to finding local work that doesn't take me away from the house for days. And, I did go back to my original dream of becoming a psychiatrist. Scarlett has brought joy back into my life, without which I wouldn't be able to function. Her first puppy cut was yesterday, so now she looks like a proper giant schnauzer. I'm focused on Scarlett at the moment, but will also adopt an airedale terrier at some point, calling him Rhett.

Scarlett looked at me with a turning head. The alarm clock went off at six, but I slept until seven when my health alert alarm went off to notify me that I needed to log my weight so that I can lose weight.

"Scarlett, we slept in."

I put on my blue, fuzzy robe in a freezing cold house even though it is summer and slid into my slippers, swaying back and forth to the kitchen, picking up a can of food along the way, so that I can feed Scarlett.

"Come on. Go outside."

Scarlett runs down the back steps, and disappears into the yard, looking for places to relieve herself. I prepare her meal, and place the large dog food bowl down.

"Okay, Scarlett, come back in. Come on."

Scarlett returns to the kitchen, sniffs her food, and then goes to the living room where she finds toys to play with.

"Scarlett, go get your breakfast. Winston. Come on. Do you want your chew?"

I get up off of the couch and go get the chicken jerky strip for Scarlett, along with a dental chew. She eats both, and then goes to her dog bowl, finishing only the soft food while leaving a large amount of kibble in the container.

"Okay, Scarlett. Let's go for a walk."

Early morning is still hot, but Scarlett doesn't care. I change clothes, put on my walking shoes, and grab

Scarlett's electric shock collar that keeps her in the invisible fence and I take it off. I put Scarlett's red walking collar on, and clip the leash to the ring on the collar. We begin to walk down the rocky drive and head left, down the hill that we will climb back up.

"Good, girl, Scarlett."

Scarlett begins to pull down the hill, stopping in shady spots to catch a few moments of relief from the scorching morning sun. It is August, and the dog days of summer have come. We continue on down the hill, however, turning around at the end of the road and beginning the climb back up the hill.

"God, it's hot," I say, out of breath.

Pausing under every tree that provides substantial shade, Scarlett and I make it back to the house where she drinks half a bowl of water. I go to the landfill and to get hay with my father, return, and Scarlett is on another walk with my mother and C. C. I go down the driveway to greet them, and Scarlett pulls the leash away from my mother's grip and begins to jump on me as a greeting. I reach down, grab the leash, and we walk up the gravel drive. Scarlett drinks a hoard of water again, and we all go inside where Scarlett takes her mid-morning nap. I write. It's nearly noon, and I have to wake Scarlett up, feed her, and take her for yet another walk. The day will be long. We'll retire around eight o'clock tonight, with Scarlett sleeping on the bed. We'll wake up at the same time tomorrow. It will go like this until I get paid on the first of the month, allowing for me to take Scarlett on hikes over the weekends.

It's 6:30am. I wake up and Scarlett is already being cared for by my parents. The days have started to blur together and she is growing fast. We hike. We walk. We play. Scarlett is understanding of my occasional mood swings due to my mental illness, calming me with little black eyes. I still dream that Jack, Russell and Philippe are alive. They're not, of course. I can't let them go. Their shrine is still in the bedroom and I wake up to it every morning. Scarlett has begun to replace them, however. We do everything together, even shopping. My fairy tale happened. My life changed for the better because of Scarlett. Everything shines now. I've realized that I have to accept the process of life, especially the lives of animals, children with fur. I will never forget Jack, Russell and Philippe. But, I have to move on. And, dear reader, I hope that you've taken this journey with me and realized that your fur babies are more important than you, and need to be cared for.

Printed in the United States
by Baker & Taylor Publisher Services